Sins We Love

pride

SINS

envy

We Love

anger

Embracing Brokenness, Hoping for Wholeness

sloth

RANDY L. ROWLAND

greed

gluttony

DOUBLEDAY

New York London Toronto Sydney Auckland

lust

PUBLISHED BY DOUBLEDAY
a division of Random House, Inc.
1540 Broadway, New York, New York 10036

DOUBLEDAY and the portrayal of an anchor with a dolphin are
trademarks of Doubleday, a division of Random House, Inc.

Library of Congress Cataloging-in-Publication Data
Rowland, Randy L.
Sins we love: embracing brokenness, hoping for wholeness.—1st ed.
p. cm.
1. Deadly sins. I. Title.
BV4626.R69   2000
241′.3—dc21   00-026204

ISBN 0-385-49703-2
Copyright © 2000 by Randy L. Rowland
All Rights Reserved
Printed in the United States of America
July 2000
First Edition

1   3   5   7   9   10   8   6   4   2

BOOK DESIGN BY JENNIFER ANN DADDIO

*Sins We Love is dedicated
to all those spiritual pilgrims
who live the present pain of brokenness,
eschewing despair for the great hope
of becoming whole by the grace of God.*

Acknowledgments

In attempting to write a book one learns early on that every book has a team that brings it to fruition. I want to thank my entire team.

I thank God for the gift of life and ability to choose. I thank my two children, Rachel and Andrew, for giving me space to write this book. My best friend, Nancy Rowland, is the world's best proofreader and grammarian and a very good editor. She shapes my intuitive musings into proper English. Nancy is also a source of patience and encouragement, without which I could not have attempted this project. I want to thank my dad for being my friend, a personal hero, and a steady presence in my life. My deepest thanks to my agent, Sara Fortenberry, who has been invaluable on the business side of things, and to my cheerleader, Lonnie Hull Dupont, a friend who has encouraged my writing. I want to thank my editor, Eric Major at Doubleday, for excessive doses of patience and encouragement. Editing is a fine art. Anyone who can make my writing understandable is an artist like Leonardo da Vinci.

The people of Church at the Center in Seattle, Washington, also deserve a lot of credit. This book originated as a sermon series. Gracious members of the congregation helped me develop ideas on the topic of sin—and they have freed me up to do this writing. Thanks a million.

As is always the case in works of this sort, all the really good stuff comes from those named above and a host of others. All flaws are the author's unique contributions.

Foreword

Reading this marvelous book by Randy Rowland has served as an important reality check for me. I happened to read the manuscript right after I participated in a public dialogue with a Buddhist and a Hindu. We were talking about promoting peace in the world, and I agreed with my two fellow panelists that the topic is indeed an important one. While we Christians have a clear mandate from our Lord to serve as peacemakers in the world, I said, the task of peacemaking is greatly complicated by the fact of sin. We are ourselves sinners, as the Apostle James reminded the early church: "Those conflicts and disputes among you, where do they come from?" he asked. "Do they not come from your cravings that are at war within you?" (James 4:1) And it isn't enough simply to deal with our own personal sinfulness. Needless to say, we also face a larger world that is caught up in the complex cursedness of our fallen condition.

Well, my "needless to say" line highlighted something that was not at all obvious to my two fellow panelists. They made it clear that they operate with a very different view of the basic problem of the human condition. The Buddhist was the one who made the response, but the Hindu nodded her head vigorously in agreement with his point: "There is no such thing as original sin. There is only original ignorance!" We spent the next part of our discussion exploring our differences on this subject. I sensed that a few folks in the audience—a gathering on a university campus—agreed with my analysis. But it also seemed obvious that most of the crowd was on the side of the proponents of "spiritual enlightenment" as the solution to our basic human problems.

As I drove home I was a bit discouraged. The fact of our sinfulness is such an important element in the Christian message. Yet it seems that people are often desperate to accept any other diagnosis of what it is that ails us as human beings, just as long as it does not require us to acknowledge that we have rebelled against the God who created us. While it is widely proclaimed these days that we in the West are living in a post-modern age, for many of our contemporaries that simply means that we need to trade in one kind of "enlightenment" for another, as people turn away from secular humanism to Eastern or New Age prescriptions for overcoming the ignorance that is seen as the root cause of our individual and collective brokenness.

I'm glad that the *Sins We Love* manuscript was waiting for me when I arrived home. Reading this book renewed my spirit. I came away with my understanding of original sin, and how it can be proclaimed in our contemporary context, enriched and expanded. Randy Rowland is a marvelous missiologist. His book is "contextualized" theology at its best—culturally savvy, evangelistically motivated, pastorally sensitive. His understanding of sin is solidly grounded in classical orthodoxy, and at the same time it speaks with power to people who are up to their eyeballs in contemporary North American culture. No one can match Randy Rowland in weaving together a narrative that draws on a scene from a Hollywood film, a line from a heavy metal piece, a Phyllis Diller joke, an NFL anecdote—and then a quote from Karl Barth as the punch line.

But *Sins We Love* also got through to me on a deeper level. As I read along I realized that the focus on sins—the plural form—was troubling me. I like to think about "sin" in the singular. In good Calvinist fashion I take a kind of perverse delight in detecting the original sin that works just beneath the surface of all of our human dealings, including my own sinfulness. But when we start talking about "sins" I get uneasy. Sin as a generic reality is fairly easy for my soul to handle, but the plural form gets a little too personal. And it really gets bad when we start to name the actual varieties: pride, envy, anger, sloth, greed, lust. Oh, and did I forget to mention gluttony? Sorry!

This is an important book for everyone who cares about how the Gospel of Jesus Christ still speaks to the fundamental yearnings of the human spirit. It will stimulate the mind and enlarge the understanding. But it will also speak words of correction and comfort to the secret places of our lives, where hungers lurk that too often distract us from the deeper yearnings that can only be satisfied by fellowship with the Living God.

—Richard J. Mouw
President
Fuller Theological Seminary

Contents

How to Read This Book

Every book is a unique compilation of ideas and is meant to be read in its own way. Thoreau used to refer to books as friends with whom he had dialogue.

I like this idea of dialoguing with a book—marking margins, underlining points that stick out, asking questions, and highlighting where the reader might take issue with the author.

While I have never met a book I couldn't skim by reading the first and last chapters with brief attention to the center, I am not sure that skimming is the best way to read all books.

Sins We Love is a book about the seven deadly sins. It has many anecdotes and historical notes. But the essence of my intention for this book is not the accumulation of data in the form of increased knowledge. It's not about information, but rather my desire is for this book to be an agent of transformation in a reader's life as each one ponders the sources of virtues and vices in his or her own life.

So while skimming or a fast read of another type might be helpful, I would rather see this book read in small chunks with attention to how its material dialogues with you, the reader.

Another thing that has always been important in my educational pursuits and in my spiritual journey is community. I need others. Do you? If so, consider doing a multiweek study of this book with some friends.

However you read *Sins We Love,* I want to thank you for acquiring this book and I want to wish you all the best as you read on.

ONE

Come On,
a Book About Sin?

Sin is definitely a controversial subject. Do you believe there is such a thing as sin? Is it a legitimate problem? Maybe you do, maybe you don't, but I can tell you that there is a lot of confusion in our world about the issue of sin.

I was standing in front of a group of over one hundred people in a divorce recovery seminar sponsored by a local church. I had been asked to speak about failure and forgiveness—how to be forgiven, how to forgive, how to move on in life.

It began to go badly as soon as I opened my mouth, "We are broken people who live in a broken world. Sin and brokenness are a real part of the human condition. When people who are not whole try to make a life together, they sometimes fail. That's the concept of sin. But the great thing is that while we are in the sin business, God is involved in an even greater enterprise called forgiveness."

Scarcely had I finished this first thought when a young woman sitting almost dead center in the room rose to her feet red-faced and screamed, "Don't you call me a sinner! I am not a sinner. My husband sinned!! I never sinned. I'm not a sinner! Don't call me a sinner."

Needless to say, the meeting was a little shaky from that point forward. Several caring leaders helped this woman out of the room and listened to her story with great compassion. I had not given your typical hell-fire condemnation of the human condition, yet I had so upset this woman that she was nearly inconsolable. I felt bad that my words had hurt her. I felt bad for myself as one who was seriously misunderstood. But at an even more troubling level, I became aware that the issue of human frailty, brokenness—sin—is a very threatening subject for many of us. We tend to reserve the word "sin" for the misdeeds of others, as the woman in the seminar did. Sin is something absolute. And, frankly, we don't much like absolutes in our emerging postmodern culture.

There's hardly a one of us who doesn't imagine herself to be without sin, especially since we minimize our malfunctioning. Not only do we minimize our dysfunction, we rename it. So sin becomes what serial killers do, while we dub ourselves only slightly flawed, and self-redeemed by our good intentions.

I am convinced that sin is so real, so horrifying, and so hard to address without the help of God, that most of us play a gigantic, complex game. Full of intrigue, we execute the various moves of our game, trying to make sin a thing we can either deny or master. We fail to recognize that sin is a chronic condition. Sin influences much of what we generalize as the human condition.

Now, as with my revelatory experience at the divorce recovery group discussing the topic of sin, I realize that most of my moments of enlightenment and insights come attendant with deep embarrassment. My musings on sin had no different genesis. Perhaps I could have been a better, more skilled, and more sensitive communicator. And perhaps we have a very unclear understanding of sin. We recoil at the very word. Sin. What an outmoded term! I decide what's right and wrong for me! No one can tell me that what I do is anything other than what I declare it to be. This sort of thinking moves us from a humble and accurate view of human nature as flawed and sinful to a place where we exonerate ourselves from all personal evil. We celebrate the goodness inherent in all creatures and deny the brutality, deceit, and toxicity within us all.

After my encounter at the seminar, I began some serious reflection about human nature and about the culture we live in. It's strange: Our level of brokenness and struggle is as high as it has ever been in all of history. Students gun down classmates in high school rampages. A Seattle parent kills his daughter, shooting her with two full magazines of bullets because she gave him a look he didn't like. Racial, ethnic, and tribal fighting dominates the world news. Road rage isn't a passing phenomenon—it's a reality we always have to consider. Anger isn't just a feeling we sometimes have. Anger, real as it is, can have strong and devastating circumstances when handled poorly.

I guess I have to get personal at this point. When I see chaos, violence, and brokenness in the world, the thing that troubles me most is a creeping awareness that all of that evil is also in me. I am a sinful person. I was musing the other day that my life is a bit like a mine shaft with impressive amounts of precious ore, yet at the same time polluted by veins of dangerous toxic substances. The precious ore is overwhelming—it's the glory, the mother lode of the mine. Yet for some damnable reason, I spend much of my time distracted with that deadly toxic vein.

In the midst of all of this chaos and pain, so many of us who live on this side of the vale of tears cannot bring ourselves to acknowledge that there is a distortion in all of us that is reflected in the human condition. One explanation for this might be that the sins we commit are the sins we love. We love these sins because, even though they are finally self-destructive, they provide some immediate emotional or physical payoff that we find irresistible. These despicable sins you and I struggle with ought to be an affront to everything we stand for, yet these sins offer us ill-gotten and short-lived benefits that make them the sins we love.

As a boating enthusiast, I very much enjoy sea stories. One of the ancient tales of the sea is that of mysterious creatures known as sirens, those mythological creatures who appeared to sailors on watch. In the distance sirens looked ravishingly beautiful, but a brief glance led to fixation upon the form of the siren. The sound of their voices was a hypnotic lure that couldn't be resisted. At the point of full absorption with the glamour of the siren, sailors would jump overboard and swim to the object of their dreams. Upon arrival, they would discover an ugly, monstrous hag who would drag the sailor into the deep where he would drown and be eaten.

The Seven Deadly Sins are like sirens. They beckon us toward them as if they are indeed something lovely. We fall in love with everything about these sins. They seem to offer so much to us. But when we answer the call, investing ourselves fully in swimming and striving toward them, we find ourselves face to face with a nightmare that annihilates us.

For example, prominent voices have pronounced that "greed is good." That sounds good to us. We all want to acquire and be well off. We like the comfort, fascination, and cumulative effect of all of our toys and we love the thrill of acquisition. We acquire more and more, and enough is never enough. Greed pays short-term dividends, but is a bust as a life goal. Psychologists refer to the PIG— the principle of instant gratification. Against all knowledge of this tendency and the evil it can summon, we still rush headlong into sinful behaviors such as greed. I am still greedy. I know I shouldn't be. I don't want to be. And actually I can be very generous and modest in some regards. My house is humble. My cars are average. But my greed comes out in other ways. I want to travel and see the world before I die and I want a bigger boat and more money in my retirement account. Aren't I entitled to those things? After all, I'm

Come On, a Book About Sin?

a good person. Ludicrous. I really do possess this arrogance regarding life. Our inherent sin deceives us into believing that the things that will actually hamper us are, in fact, an entitlement.

Having goals and having material comforts are not evil in themselves. It is the distortion of these things by making them little gods, or idols, that moves them from the category of "some of life's gifts" to objects of greed and acquisition. This distortion places rightful things at a low priority and exalts less rightful things to the top of the hierarchy of priorities in life. My wants, needs, and ambitions are not pure evil. But my life and your life suffer from the distortions of making the wrong things the object of our worship.

This issue of sin is all about distortion. When God, our Creator, made the world He declared it "good." When we see the brokenness of this world, we don't have to ponder, "Why, God, why?" Instead we ought to ask, "Why, humanity, why?" That's God's question for us. God created a good and beautiful world and we have vandalized the canvas upon which God painted. Sin is a distortion of God's good creation and God's will for you and me. Perhaps I should strengthen the severity of sin by saying it is at least a distortion of the Good. Better yet, it is a perversion of the Good. Perverted love results in pride, envy, rage. Insufficient love results in sloth. Excessive love of things in this world leads to greed, gluttony, and lust.

Sin is the act of perverting what God has made. The distortions throw the various elements of life out of proper priority. God calls for us to work and be productive in order to make a better world; we turn the call to vocation into workaholism and cut a path of destruction. Jeff is a doctor. His profession is demanding to begin with. But Jeff is driven to success and approval. His work becomes his excuse for not having a life. It is his excuse for his mistakes, his relationship failures, and it is his excuse for limited involvement in a church. While the doctor heals many, he is becoming sicker and sicker in body, mind, and soul. Panic anxiety attacks, insomnia, physical aches, and poor moral choices are taking him down. Surely the proverb that reads "There is a way that seems wise to a man, but its end is destruction" applies to Jeff.

Another distortion is the misuse of God's gifts. For example, sex is a gift that provides an opportunity for procreation and intimate pleasure between faithful, lifetime partners. Even though America's sexual revolution is waning, its legacy is a twisted perception that sex is something to which we have a right, no matter the cost to ourselves and to others. And the goal of the sexual act is more about personal gratification than it is about intimacy in a committed relationship. It is the same with gluttony, the perverted desire for things of this world. This includes food, drink, and consumerism. We eat, drink, and spend ourselves to death daily in America. You don't have to look very far to find an example. A friend named Paul has a serious weight problem. It seriously threatens the longevity of his life. He is still quite young. Many of us can relate to the struggle with weight. But Paul is unique in this struggle, because he has given up. His body is being destroyed because he is extremely overweight and ignores treatment for his diabetes; now he needs a motorized wheelchair to get around. Paul has distorted the purpose of food and drink in his life with the result that these life-giving gifts from God are the cause of his demise.

Wrong prioritization and wrong use of God-given gifts that are part of the Creation are bad enough, but there is yet one more effect of the distortion. For some reason, human beings have inherited a twisted bent in which we all desire to be God. Instead of revering one loving God who rules graciously over His Creation, we have forgotten God and try to maintain order in a world with over 5 billion people who all consider themselves rulers. This final distortion blinds us to God and opens us to the deceitful idea that we are all there is and we are in charge.

The classical name for distortion is sin. I will share some definitions of sin in this chapter. Chances are good that the definitions of words which we translate as "sin" will be helpful in our understanding of this life-threatening condition. I don't intend to take this lack of acceptance of sin too lightly. It happens at many levels of society with a good majority of people. It even happens in seminary classes.

During my days at seminary, I had a theology professor, Sam Mikolaski, who was a first-generation Serbian refugee from the period prior to World War II. His people fled ethnic purges and he was lucky to make it out. He had seen human sin rooted in prejudice and injustice close up.

One day in our class, while Dr. Mikolaski was lecturing on the topic of sin, a student raised his hand and asserted, "I just don't believe in sin or evil the way you do. I don't think there's any such thing."

Dr. Mikolaski responded passionately: "I have stood outside the gates of Bergen-Belsen concentration camp and have sifted through my hands the sediment that is the cremated remains of hundreds of thousands of innocent human lives. Don't tell me there is no such thing as evil. I have seen the evidence of evil." Evil is a real thing. Sin is ever present in a broken world. It is hardly a matter to be discounted or taken lightly, especially when we consider events like the Holocaust or the ethnic cleansing that is a part of so many conflicts even today.

If evil is real, why do we so often gloss over it or deny it? If we don't acknowledge a problem, that doesn't mean it doesn't exist or that it will go away soon if ignored. If I suffer from a chronic disease, I should know all that I can about my malady and do everything I am able to manage it. Living in denial or ignorance serves only to amplify the profound ill effects of the condition in the long term.

The Creator designed the universe and the social order that works within the universe. The underlying principles of science and morality work best when linked to the Creator as the source of all truth and perfection and possibilities. There is a blueprint for life. God expresses that blueprint in nature and in the Scriptures, providing a set of "channel markers" by which we may navigate. I realize blueprints and navigational markers might sound like a mixed metaphor, but consider this: Every waterway, be it sea, bay, or river, has a blueprint, a signature, a design that defines "the way it is." Skilled people in the Coast Guard determine the natural blueprint of channels and mark them with buoys to enlighten ships' navigators and boaters. To deny the reality of a channel and disregard the markers is an act of extreme foolishness. I will demonstrate why first using the Bible and then with a hair-raising story.

The Apostle John had fascinating insights into the nature of human sinfulness and the graciousness of God. His formula for our behavior when we encounter sin in our lives, outlined in his first epistle, is absolutely practical and it has stood the test of time for twenty centuries. The reason that this text is so powerful is not merely its human wisdom, but because it is God's actual words revealed to us through His servant, John. The Apostle says, "If we say we have no sin, we deceive ourselves and call God a liar. If we confess our sin, God is faithful and just. God forgives our sin and returns us to wholeness and good standing with Him."

The formula is as follows: If we confess sins, things turn for the positive. It results in our gracious God forgiving us. And our forgiving God wipes the slate clean and gives us a new start.

This is the rhythm of a grace-filled life—to own our failures and hold them up to a God who loves us more than He could possibly hate the sins we have committed. This is a God who not only forgives our shortcomings but also expends awesome spiritual resources on you and me to restore us body and soul. If this is such a good deal, why do we so often turn it down and live in denial?

If we deny brokenness and sin, the following two things happen: First, self-deceit sets in. It's deadly. It's the beginning of the end of the examined life. Down through time, philosophers and sages have said that the unexamined life is not worth living. Second, God, who declares all His human creatures beloved and precious in spite of their flaws, gets called a liar for saying that one behavior or another is a sin.

When I consider the negative ramifications of John's formula, I actually see a hint into the very nature and location of sin: the human ego. Self-deceit is the indulgence we offer ourselves when we are fabulous in our own eyes. We grant ourselves little "gimmes" and in so doing assert that we alone rule over our own life. Welcome to the wild, wild west and radical individualism.

Another aspect of the denial of sin comes if we call God a liar. Again, look at the heart of that action and we get a glimpse of the heart of sin. Calling God a liar is saying, "No one will decide anything for me. I am my own authority." We place ourselves on dangerous ground when we become our own authority. Most of us who are followers of Jesus Christ and believe that the Bible is the revealed Word of God find ourselves repulsed at the idea of a human being usurping God's rightful role with the assertion of self as a god or at least the source of theology. Yet, while we believe this with all of our minds, our souls fall prey to sin.

Rosemary was a married woman. She was raising several children with a husband who had a responsible job and was a pretty good life partner. For some unknown reason, Rosemary went out of control.

Her first foray into a self-destructive lifestyle began with some visits to a local bar with girlfriends on a weekly girls' night out.

Many of her companions were single. She met a lot of men at the bars, and as you would probably suspect, before long she was committing adultery.

Rosemary believes every single word and teaching of Scripture is the authoritative Word of God. She knows adultery is outside of God's channel markers for life. But, to my amazement, I watched her create a scenario to rationalize her behavior. She said, "God loves me and wants me to have a fulfilling life. That means I don't have to be stuck with someone who bores me and whom I may not love anymore. This is my time to discover the real me that God has created me to be." It was as if she had become spiritually numb. She denied the rule of God over her life in order to follow what she felt were matters of the heart. Denial of sin and of God's authority can easily corrupt an entire worldview. Rosemary actually began to think that she was the victim of a bad life that her husband was inflicting upon her.

Interestingly, the denial of sin and the questioning of God's reliability throw a double wedge into the works. First of all, we anesthetize ourselves to the need for correction and personal renewal when we practice the self-deceit of denying sin. Our conscience, which functions like a smoke alarm in our lives, is rendered useless like a smoke alarm with worn-out batteries. Then, in our need to justify ourselves, we allow a rift to grow in our relationship with a gracious and loving God, who wants nothing but the best for us. We go on life's voyage denying the knowledge and assistance of a Creator who kindly marks the channel on which we navigate.

As I've said, I am a boater. I love being on the water as often as possible. When I go boating, I am forced to be very conscious of channel markers. At several places on Puget Sound in Washington State, there are narrow channels bounded by shallow reefs or sandbars. Interestingly, people often gamble. If the tide is high enough, they cut a corner to save time and skim over the underwater hazards. It works a lot of the time and many boaters feel that they are ahead of the pack for doing this. On the other hand, several times a year, someone miscalculates and is left grounded, wrecked, or even sunk.

One such incident became a parable for life for my family. We were cruising south from the San Juan Islands in an area near the Skagit River delta. The channel is graciously wide, but a line of red buoys cautions thinking boaters to stay to the west of the buoys. As we cruised away, enjoying the sun, a thirty-foot speedboat zoomed across our wake and to the east. The folks aboard the boat were whooping it up and hoisting beer cans (not their first cans, I suspected). When I honked trying to tell them that they were outside the channel, they returned an obscene gesture. They were moving at about 35 mph into a boater's nightmare.

About half a mile ahead of us these happy-go-lucky, "I determine my own boundaries and channel markers" folks hit a sand flat wedging the boat, throwing passengers and other boat contents all over the place. Going over to help them would have endangered other boats too near the sandbar. No one was hurt, so they simply had to wait about nine hours for the tide to go out and come back in again and lift them off the hazard.

Our Creator desires wholeness for us. Warnings and prohibitions against certain negative behaviors are not meant to restrict us, but rather to keep us safe and well. We must get over the idea of rules and morality being oppressive and begin to see them as invitations to freedom and wholeness. "Don't kill" is a life-nurturing command from the Creator. It is no different than the life-nurturing directive we give our young children, "Don't play in the street or you might get hit by a car."

In spite of the good-intentioned nature of God's blueprint for life, we humans fancy the idea that we can find a better way. What is it in us that makes us act this way? Well, it's probably one part resisting being told what to do by anyone, including God. Second, it may have to do with our desire to be in total control. While Frank Sinatra popularized the song "My Way," some of the other singers of a similar song have shown that "my way" has ramifications beyond the "me" involved at the center of a choice being made. Adolf Hitler and Joseph Stalin, Pol Pot and Mao Tse-tung all sang their own "My Way." That's the insidiousness of this distortion of the human condition. When we measure how it "works for me," we fail to get a clear picture of the overall effects of sin. Sin and righteousness both have an impact on the entire social and created order. When we measure our actions by "My Way," we diminish or deny our interdependency with Creator, Creation, and creatures.

Sin. What is its effect? Sin rips at the fabric of God's good Creation. Sin is a part of human nature. And sin is a real problem. Whether you read Greek classics or today's Patricia Cornwell or John Grisham novels, you will encounter the concept of sin. Sin is an inseparable part of our human condition, taking many forms. Let me share just a few definitions from the Judeo-Christian understanding of sin. I won't get technical with ancient dead languages but I will, however, offer definitions of the numerous terms used for sin in classical literature, including the texts of the Old and New Testaments.

Sin means to "miss the mark." Imagine shooting at a target on a range. Each time you miss the bull's-eye, you are a sinner. Sin means "nice try, but you missed."

Sin also means "straying or wandering" from the correct path. A better image for this is "to slip." Imagine walking on a snow-covered sidewalk when suddenly you place your foot on a patch of ice and find yourself on the ground with a sore backside. At least two New Testament words for sin imply a failure of a lesser order. Failure to hit the bull's-eye is a good effort gone bad. A slip on the ice is an unexpected event that caution may have preempted.

Sin is moral decadence. In this regard, the person who denies the reality of sin and does nothing to protect himself against its effects becomes a victim of his own sin and that of others, resulting in serious moral erosion. Sometimes our denial of sin comes from a sincere motive of self-protection. In the end, the result is self-destruction.

Sin is injustice. Doing somebody less than "right" is all wrong. It's a breach in the relationship between the offender and the one done the injustice—a breach of the relationship between a loving God and the Creation and the creatures God has made. Sin is not private. Its systemic results are an unjust society.

Sin is rebellion. By rebellion I mean not only a proclamation of self-sufficiency for the sake of personal freedom but also an intentional effort to behave in ways that sabotage or undermine the way things ought to be. This is the corruptive force that claims moral free agency, yet creates quite a bondage. One very literary singer/songwriter portrayed rebellion as a marionette who, hoping to be free, cuts its own strings. We all know that such action doesn't result in freedom—rather it leaves just a pile on the floor.

Sin is deliberate perversion. This state of sin has to do with intentionally doing what is wrong in order to make a mockery of righteousness, or what is right. The goal is to undermine and rip the very fabric of the social order and personal health.

These six different renderings of the word sin are very helpful in describing the global nature of the problem. I am far from being a great human being, but as I look down this list, which increases in severity, I can pretty well exempt myself from the last three kinds of sins almost all the time. So, I'm a good guy, right? Not really. I find myself missing the mark (see definition one) and slipping (definition two) all the time.

Now, here's the rub: If you've committed one of the sins I've listed, you have committed them all. Each corrupts and distorts hu-

man life, self-awareness, the social order, and our disposition toward Creation. If I say I am morally better than others who have
more sin points against them, doesn't that make me superior? According to classic philosophers like Aristotle and great Christian
thinkers throughout the centuries, the answer is no. The great majority of the renowned thinkers in the sin/virtue arena agree that
any corruption is total corruption. In the same manner, we cannot
assume that we are good because we are less bad than someone else
to whom we choose to compare ourselves. If I say that I can swim
twenty miles and boast that I can outperform all other swimmers,
then dive into the ocean off the California coast in a swimming race
to Hawaii, my end-state will equal all the others: I will drown.
Where's the glory in drowning last? Comparisons with others in the
issue of sin is a fruitless argument. It may actually help lead to our
downfall because it can make us not take our own sins nearly seriously enough. Our broken, sinful nature is so serious and so real,
that we cannot become smug about it or say, "Well, at least I didn't
ever murder anyone." We are all miles short of the goodness and
wellness that the Creator envisions for us. Each of us has set out to
drown in our sea of chaos and corruption. When we don't compare,
we often get caught playing the blame game and pointing the finger
at others and their sins.

We find comfort in pointing out the sins in others. My wife and
I learned this the hard way. We were going through some struggles
in our relationship a number of years ago and decided to go see a
counselor. For several weeks, the counselor listened to each of us
complain about each other and define our issues. The shock to us
came when the therapist said, "Your homework before the next ses-
sion is to go home and write down what you bring to this marriage
that makes it difficult at times. We'll compare notes next time and
see what things each of you can take responsibility for changing."
We both had thought the other one would need to do the changing!

Among the inescapable truths about sin is that it is insidious, powerful, and harmful. Like the rippling effect of a single stone cast in the water, the consequences of sin go far beyond our own ability to comprehend. When I was a kid, I was told that if you shine a flashlight into the sky and then turn it off, you haven't stopped the beam of light it just emitted from traveling across the universe. So it is with sin—our moral failings have a life of their own. They multiply and breed with other failures in a continuing cycle. I say I don't like a certain group of people and that I am entitled to my opinion, what's the harm in that? Well, when my kids pick up my attitude and rhetoric, they become prejudiced and discriminatory. Support my sinful attitude for a few generations and you will build systems of enslavement and racial inequality that become part of our society, or plant the seeds of evils like recently abolished apartheid in South Africa.

So, the best place to begin considering sin is not in our society, not in those around us, but rather in ourselves. It's there. Inside me. Inside you. It takes some courage to face. But as we face the reality of sin in our lives, we also face the reality of increasing wholeness, internal peace, and more fulfilling relations with others. I have often asked myself, "Rowland, why do you sin so much? When you try to be good you sin, and when you want to sin intentionally, you are absolutely brilliant in your capacity to do so."

For me, it comes down to human ego—the assertion of my will, the assertion of my will above all else. I also see it as the worship of convenience and instinct over active spirituality. It's so subtle. I can demonstrate by way of example. I am a fairly law-abiding citizen. I tend to obey traffic signs and signals. But, for some reason, I despise the private traffic signs that stores put up saying "no right turn" or "no left turn." I flagrantly ignore them. Now, why do I do this? It's a form of arrogance. I assert that I know traffic planning better than the parking lot designers. And I simultaneously assert that I am just a little better than everyone else, and while that sign is for "him or her" it doesn't apply to me. I am special. What I am is a sinner. I need help. This stuff is personal and powerful. Exploring sin in our lives is tremendously threatening. We might feel threatened and defensive as well. Actually, that's good. It means that we are taking the topic seriously.

It is my hope that you will take this book, first and foremost, as a personal journey. What does it have to say to you? How might you want to adjust your worldview to adequately account for the fallen nature of human beings? What resolutions for moral and spiritual renewal might you make?

And do be mindful as you read that where there is sin, there is also forgiveness, just by asking God for cleansing. This sounds easy on paper, but it's against our nature to be wrong or to be vulnerable in any way, shape, or form. Reinhold Niebuhr, a noted ethicist early in the last century, said, "Mankind's sin lies in the pretension to be God."

So, like the marionettes who reach up and cut the strings that enable and direct them, we lay crumpled and broken on the stage of life. The job God holds as Ruler of the Universe has not been open for any new applicants. Yet we try to usurp God's role as Creator. And we fail. And we mess up our lives. And we mess up the world.

But even from our place of pain and failure, we can look to a God who is capable of restoring us. Listen to this poetic assertion by God through the voice of the prophet Isaiah (Isaiah 43:25, 26a):

"I, even I, am he who blots out your transgressions, for my own sake, and remembers your sins no more. Review the past for me, let us argue the matter together."

The good news about the bad news of sin is that God is bigger and better than any sin we can manufacture. And there is no sin God cannot forgive.

God is willing to forgive, restore, and remove the guilt of sin, so long as we are willing to name it for what it is, claim responsibility for our actions, and seek cleansing. This predisposition to blot out wrongs and renew our spiritual center is called grace. Grace emanates from a loving God who goes to great extremes to hang on to us and nurture our lives.

For those familiar with the Christian story, we learn of a God who jumps into a human costume and lives among us, experiencing all the pain and joys and temptations of real life. That God's name is Jesus. The Christian story goes on to record the fact that Jesus died a criminal's death under the Roman justice system in order to restore a right relationship between God and human beings.

As I mentioned earlier, sin tears at the fabric of God's perfect Creation. God is not in the business of destroying the agents of corruption. God loves you and me beyond our ability to comprehend. Nothing we can say or do will ever get God to love us more. And God is "for" us and "with" us and even "in us" by the Holy Spirit as we strive to align ourselves with the blueprint of life and begin a global process of mending, or darning, the fabric of Creation, torn by what we call sin.

This repair work is called reconciliation. Our English word comes from a Latin word meaning "to restore to friendship or harmony." It's literally the image of setting and mending a broken bone, or repairing a knitted article of clothing. Isn't that an exciting concept? Rather than participate in the undoing of things—the tearing of the fabric—we are invited to renew our own lives and actively work in partnership with God and others to restore what is ruined.

I find the invitation extended to you and me by our Creator, to be active agents in this reconciliation process, to be absolutely overwhelming. I have trouble at times believing that the God whom I have offended is anxious to forgive me, fix me, and utilize me to further spread his love and grace in the world. That God can use our lives to repair the distortions and return love, beauty, and goodness to all of Creation is a fascinating invitation into a meaningful life of work and social interaction. I reckon it to be the adventure of a life-time. In fact, this destiny is the very thing for which you and I are created. We have fears that have paralyzed us. We have wounds that have maimed us. In spite of these, being a cocreator with God in the New Creation led by Jesus Christ is what most of us really, really desire. Sin stands in our way. How can we help save a world from its sins if we cannot at least manage our own sins? That's what this book is about: identifying sin and exploring ways to keep it in check.

Please note carefully my comment about keeping sin in check. From my theological perspective, sin is and always will be a prob-lem for every human being. The distortion is so great, we can never escape it fully, but we can wrestle with it and develop spiritual practices that mediate against sin's effects.

In some thoughtful and well-meaning theological traditions, there is a sincere belief that we can purify ourselves from sin and escape sin's gravity. This is called Christian perfection, which is the end of a process called sanctification. (I discuss the terms holy and holiness later in this book.) But holiness and sanctification are in-tertwined. To either be sanctified or holy means to be set apart. They are very important words, and misunderstanding or misapply-ing them can result in emotional and spiritual disasters.

As followers of Jesus Christ, Christians are being set apart con-stantly in a personal renewal process that might be termed a moral and spiritual evolution. In my reformed tradition, where I resonate with theologians like John Calvin, John Knox, Charles Hodge, and Karl Barth, we respect the dignity of other viewpoints, but we ourselves have a fairly pessimistic view of human nature. Each of these great thinkers was awestruck at the tremendous potential of all humans because we are created in the image of God. Yet, at the same time, each of the great theologians was aghast at the propensity of evil and destruction latent within each of us. Out of these dual observations of a possibility for good and a penchant for evil, the great theological minds in Christian history have focused on managing and reducing the penchant for evil by recognizing that everyone and everything is broken.

Along with some pretty formidable theological colleagues throughout history, I have to admit that I believe in sanctification, and hold to the idea that every Christian will someday be sanctified and perfected. And I am happy to announce that this will take place the very day you and I enter heaven. But on this side of heaven, we are left to battle and ward off the death, decay, and humiliation of sin, but are never free from it. To say we can be free of sin in a sinful world would be like saying to someone living in Hong Kong or Los Angeles that they will soon arrive at a place of personal development where they will not have to breathe polluted air. Sorry. We're here. And it's a bit of a mess. To draw the pollution concept out a little farther, what is really troubling is not just that the pollution is in the air, but that it is in our minds, our hearts, our habits. And we have to come to a point of confession where we admit that sins we commit so regularly and with such cavalier disregard, or even callous bragging, are committed because they are the sins we love.

As you read this book and do personal inventories, don't forget the positive. Acknowledging sin and asking for forgiveness of sin are just a start. The real adventure is in living lives of substance within the virtues. Our lives and our actions matter. We can start movements of goodness, kindness, gentleness, and generosity right here and right now. We all desire to love and be loved. As we move through and beyond the sins we love, we move toward the absolute love we need.

Join me as we study the numerous manifestations of this disease called Sin, and consider the many hygienic responses that mediate against sin's Creation-crushing effects. The Seven Deadly Sins are our guide in understanding the underside of human nature, but they also enliven us to the incredible possibilities of a life of virtue, lived in the power of the Holy Spirit.

TWO

The Seven Deadly Sins

In the sixth century of the Christian era, a very influential figure emerged. His name was Gregory. In fourteen years as the Bishop of Rome, Gregory presided in leadership over the majority of the Christian church. Known to us now as Gregory the Great, he became pope in the year 590.

Gregory was a fabulous thinker and a bold leader who also suffered greatly. He was afflicted with numerous ailments that often left him at death's door. He was a man quite in tune with his own limitations, flaws, and struggles. Yet, he worked tirelessly to serve his Lord and the Church over which he was see.

Perhaps his own flawed body, wracked by gout and fevers, led him into a deep inner search for his own true nature. We all possess good and evil. Gregory found both good and evil in himself. He was familiar with some of the writings and sayings of the early church fathers, was familiar with the Greco-Roman worldview largely shaped by Aristotle, and, of course, he was adept in the Scriptures of the Old and New Testaments. I can almost imagine Gregory, in pain, reading Psalm 139 and saying aloud, "Search me, God, try my heart, observe my anxious thoughts and see if there is any wickedness within me." I am somewhat boldly speculating here that the categorization of sins and the discussion thereof comes directly out of Gregory's own spiritual journey combined with all the other written work in the area of sin and virtue.

Gregory the Great was fascinated by discussions of virtues and vices that had taken place over time. He further developed a free-floating idea that there were clusters of virtues and clusters of sins. By addressing the sins, Gregory believed fertile ground was developed in which the seeds of virtue could grow. By cataloging sins into cluster areas, a person could more easily attempt self-examination and identify problem areas. Gregory the Great was not on a personal rampage of mind control and religious oppression. He was, by all historical accounts, a bighearted and good man who was himself on a journey toward wholeness that he wanted to share with others.

So, out of his familiarity with Aristotle (of whom Gregory was not fond), Paul, and other thinkers, Gregory assembled a sin list which we know as the Seven Deadly Sins: Pride, Envy, Anger, Sloth, Greed, Gluttony, and Lust. Each of these sin groupings represents a constellation of attitudes and behaviors, all of which destroy, hence their name "Deadly."

For Gregory, the issue of sin is that it is fatal. Romans tells us that "the wages of sin is death. . . ." I am quite sure he took this very seriously. And he gave us a very solid model. Whenever the Church of Jesus Christ or an individual Christian fails to take sin seriously, a moral erosion sets in that eventually makes sin a companion rather than an enemy. I said this earlier—sin is a chronic condition. It does not go away, and saying one does not have it will not make it go away.

This example was very difficult for me to witness as a college student. A very gifted athlete on our football team was an insulin-dependent diabetic. He decided that if he just had a positive attitude and practiced healthy self-talk, he would no longer be diabetic. He quit using insulin. Several days later, he was found near death in a diabetic coma on his apartment floor. Thank God, he was rescued. Now, let's parallel this unfortunate event with our own conceptualization of sin. We don't like the word sin. We dread many of the sinful acts we commit. And we want it to go away. We yearn to control ourselves and be our "true self." Assuming we can fully expunge the chronic condition of sin allows us to go off the spiritual medicine we need in order to survive. We see the symptoms of sin and we write them off as not really being our true self and we try to move forward, but are bound by the polluting effects of the sin in our lives.

It is, in my opinion, the chronic nature of sin that is most ignored by Christians. We hate to say, "I am a sinner. I need a savior." It sounds weak and dependent to say such things. But even more insidious is the lack of urgency. Like the college athlete who stopped using insulin, we can feel pretty good for quite a while without sticking, poking, and prodding ourselves to investigate the sinful behaviors in our lives. In the end, we begin to go dull, lose our spiritual bearings and sensibilities, and drift off into a state of unawareness. These sins are deadly over the long haul. When the Great Enemy of all souls can distract us from the seriousness of sin, he is able to reduce the urgency of sin and allow us to deepen negative behavior patterns.

There is a fictional story about three apprentice devils who are about to go to earth and corrupt humanity. They report to Satan to tell of their plans. The first devil reports that he will tell humans that there is no God. Satan tells him that will never work and sends him back to where he came from. A second apprentice steps up and says that he will tell them there is no heaven or hell. Satan again rejects the plan, telling the aspiring devil that humans know better than that. The third and final apprentice devil comes to Satan and says, "I will simply tell them that nothing is urgent." To this, the author of evil says, "Go now. Go quickly. You will ruin them by the thousands."

That is why Gregory's work is very important. He makes the issues of sin universal and urgent. He places the sins within categories that we can understand and work with. We will be discussing the key to sin management as this book moves along, but for now I will establish that the pure love that comes from God is the soul-reviving, sin-battling treatment for sin.

Gregory and others like him saw sin as a distortion of love. Some of the distortions of love were a result of perverted love. The sins of pride, anger, and envy go in this first category. A second category of insufficient love contains the sin we know as sloth. And the third category is having too much love for things that aren't top priorities for a good life. This is the category that houses greed, gluttony, and lust.

While Gregory gave the exploration of the problem of sin much of its structure, later Christian leaders followed in a similar path. The Reformers, Calvin and Luther, in particular, believed that sin was a chronically debilitating state. Calvin declared humans suffer from total depravity, a state in which they cannot even desire to save themselves. Calvin would say that humans have fallen into some deep pit and have been seriously immobilized by the Fall. Only a gracious God who comes looking for the lost and broken could remedy the human condition.

Luther's *The Bondage of the Will* is a classic work on the gravity and absoluteness of the sin condition. To Luther, the only thing good about sin, if one can say there is anything good about sin, is that it makes us acutely aware of our need for a savior. But the broken human, whose will is bound, can scarcely act to search for a savior. Instead the wounded soul can only say "yes" to a savior who comes to us in our brokenness and asks us to say "yes" to God's absolute love and forgiveness.

While there have been some historic differences between the Roman Church and Protestants, the reality of sin and the effects of sin on the human race is not a matter of contention. Furthermore, Gregory and the Reformers had good company with the inspired voices who transmitted the Word of God to us in the texts of the Old and New Testaments. David's Psalms are full of confession of sin and unrighteousness. They plead for help from a forgiving God who offers "though your sins be as scarlet, I will make them white as snow." The Apostle Paul does a spectacular job of speaking for all human beings in Romans 7 when he tells of his battle with the chronic condition of sin that torments him, regardless of his intentions. The insult and betrayal brought upon us by sin leaves Paul exasperated. The prophet Isaiah records God Almighty saying to His people, "All your righteousness is as filthy rags . . ." Sin cannot be hidden or ignored. It cannot be glossed over by allegedly good deeds or self-affirmations. It is painfully resident in all of us.

The reality of sin's residence within humanity is not just a Christian thought. In fact, much was being said about vices and virtues even before the birth of Jesus Christ. In order to achieve an adequate understanding of the Seven Deadly Sins we must consider the context from which they emerged. Sin and righteousness are not a product of the Jewish or Christian traditions alone. In fact, Plato and Aristotle had much to say about these topics over three centuries before the Christian era began.

Aristotle did much reflection on what makes life work and not work. He had theories on economics, government, communication, and ethics. Among his many writings was a piece called *Virtues and Vices*. It was written sometime around 330 B.C. in Athens. He observed human nature. He asked questions about what makes human life noble and what makes human life villainous. Out of these reflections, he arrived at a list of seven virtues and their negative counterparts, which he called vices, or sins. He proclaimed, ". . . the virtues are objects of praise . . . while the opposites are objects of blame."

Aristotle's virtues were gentleness, courage, sobriety, self-control, righteousness, liberality, and great-spiritedness. Each represented a set of behaviors rooted deeply in the human soul. They were all about a lifetime of intentional character development and spiritual formation.

Gentleness was a character trait that was slow to anger and slow to rile others to anger. Obviously, rage, anger, bitterness, bullying, striving, enmity, and warring were the vices. Gentleness believed the best, sought the best, and encouraged the best in others. In fact, Aristotle's definition of love, as I understand it, is "to seek the highest good for another."

Aristotle viewed courage as being "undismayed by fear of death." Courage was the ability to stand for the truth at all costs. The vices, on the other hand, were cowardice, slander, lying, and gossip.

A third virtue, sobriety, had to do with tuning the inner person so that there was a decreased temptation to act out inappropriately upon the baser instincts and appetites. The vices in this area—drunkenness, sexual license, gluttony, and unbridled consumerism—made us drunk with our own power and prestige and dulled our senses to what was right and good.

Self-control was similar to sobriety. It had more to do with managing the temptations we all face which seemed stronger than we could endure, well beyond our "sobriety." Vices with which self-control did battle were lust, rage, and inappropriate self-assertion.

Righteousness is an often misused word. People think of self-righteous or "too good to be true" when they hear the word. For

Aristotle, it simply meant doing what was right—doing justice. In-justice, unrighteousness, consciously choosing the wrong—these described the vice.

Sixth on Aristotle's list of virtues was liberality. This meant to be good caretakers of the resources given us in life. "Spending rightly on fine objects" was Aristotle's idea here. Vices consisted of consumerism, materialism, wastefulness, and money squandering.

Being great-spirited was the last of Aristotle's virtues. It meant to not be "small-minded." The philosopher's invitation to the virtue of open-mindedness encouraged us to consider being open to others in the midst of very clear differences. It also meant to be open to personal reflection about our own lives as we humbly considered our good and bad fortunes.

Several centuries after Aristotle, the Christian era began. One of Christianity's first great thinkers and spokespersons was the spirit-inspired Apostle Paul. Earlier in life, he had actually perse-cuted the Christian church out of a deep loyalty to the traditional religious establishment. His loyalty changed when Jesus appeared to him in a blinding light. In his transformed life, the Apostle re-flected on the life of following God. Because of his familiarity with Greco-Roman thinking, he, like Aristotle, was interested in char-acter development. His desire for himself and for those upon whom he exerted influence was to stimulate growth in virtue.

I am sure that as Paul pondered the nature of a Spirit-enriched, fruitful life, he took a long look at the virtues of Aristotle. We know that Paul's advanced studies in his native Jewish faith were pursued in a Greco-Roman school that was very orthodox regarding the Jew-ish faith, while being very open to dialogue with the Philosophers. It has been said that all truth is God's truth. And I presume Paul saw a lot of God's truth in Aristotle's list.

Paul differed with Aristotle on at least two accounts. He did not see the virtues as something attainable by human effort. He did not see them as a direct result of any personal behavior-modification program. Paul described these virtues as the "fruit of the spirit." His words indicate that the Spirit of God working deep within the human person produces an ever-increasing crop of virtue.

Paul also regarded sin as a very serious issue. Beyond just a vice that hinders (as Aristotle might claim), sin is a deadly force in all of our lives all the time. Paul languishes in his letter to the Romans, "who will deliver me from this body of sin and death?" He is acutely aware of his powerlessness against the ravages of sin. Paul demonstrates the total grip of sin when he says in Romans, "but I am unspiritual, sold as a slave to sin. I do not understand what I do. For what I want to do, I do not do, but what I hate I do." Paul marvelously sums up what it means to be human; sinful to the core.

Paul's understanding of the depths of sin is outdone only by his understanding of the grace of God. For Paul, the hope, the Good News, amid the bad news of sin is that in Jesus Christ, the Risen One, we have the power to become new. This power of the Holy Spirit comes from outside us. Paul's view of the Spirit of God's work in our life is that the Spirit brings all the resources needed for life and faith—including the same power that raised Jesus from the dead. Listen to the passion in Paul's letter to the Philippians: "I want to know Christ and the power of his resurrection . . . and so, somehow to attain the resurrection from the dead."

For Paul, the saving presence of God by the power of the Holy Spirit is the only hope for human wholeness. But it's a great big, huge, gigantic hope! Paul places the weight of his sin problem on Jesus, of whom Paul said, "He who knew no sin became sin on our behalf." The sin problem is serious. So is God's intervention.

But how does God work against the power of sin in your life and mine? What might we expect as we journey through life battling the devastating effects of sin? The secret to success may be both a comfort and a torment. The comfort comes from knowing that our lives, as Christians, are in God's hands and that God is doing something beautiful in each of us. And we can be assured by Paul's words in Philippians: "He who began a good work in you will bring it to completion on the day of Christ Jesus." Isn't it wonderful to know that God is in charge and that in the end, it will be okay? George Washington's—the first President of the United States—last two words before dying from a serious case of strep throat were, " 'Tis all right." We can live in the confession of faith that " 'tis all right." Take great comfort in this truth.

But as we cling with one hand to hope, the other hand holds the torment of the journey. The fact is that sin cannot be cured in this life. We will always need a savior. Sin can only be managed. And it cannot be fixed in short order. Rather, it's a long and winding road of triumphs and failures. It's the road toward God. One does not cover much ground at any given time. Change is slow, almost imperceptible. I am personally tormented by not being perfect. How about you? I wonder why I cannot exercise one day and be in shape, diet one day and be down to my desired weight, think beautiful thoughts one day and overcome anger and jealousy. I want it all right now.

Paul, full of the Spirit of God, tells us that we can't have perfection now, but we can start on a pathway toward wholeness now— and we can do so with the resident power of the Spirit that raised Jesus from the dead.

Early in his ministry, Paul wrote a letter to the churches of Galatia (called Galatians), which is considered by many to be his greatest work. He extols the power and grace of God, condemns religiosity as an appealing but powerless option for living, and he pronounces the freedom to be everything God dreams for us to be by the power of the Holy Spirit.

As the letter to the Galatians soars and pulses toward a magnificent crescendo, Paul introduces the concept of the fruit of the
Spirit.

Galatians 5:22, 23 reads: "The fruit of the Spirit is love, joy,
peace, patience, kindness, goodness, faithfulness, gentleness and
self-control." I am convinced that a proper reading of this text
based upon modern translation methods is: "The fruit of the Spirit
is *love*—which expresses itself as joy, peace, patience, kindness,
goodness, faithfulness, gentleness, and self-control."

The fruit of the Spirit is love. Each of the Seven Deadly Sins occurs as a result of good love gone bad. Sin is a distortion of perfect
love. The fruit of the Spirit works against the power of decay by im-
printing the perfect love of God on our very essence. That same perfect love takes root in our essence and grows outward, transforming
us, Paul says, "from one state of glory to another into the image of
Christ." I think it is fair to say that all virtue is summed up in the
single word love. If this is true, then the fruit of the Spirit (or even
Aristotle's virtues) are facets of the greater reality of love. Love is
the virtue of all virtues.

The fruit of the Spirit is love, which grows within us and mani-
fests itself in our moral being. Love sprouts joy, peace, patience,
gentleness, self-control, and all the other fruit. Love expresses itself in Technicolor through these magnificent manifestations of
God's absolute and perfect love working within us. We literally, by
the Holy Spirit, are partakers of the Life of God Himself.

Our war with sin is not waged alone. The ugliness, the vileness,
the toxic waste is not conquered by the human will or by a single
dose of grace from God. Sin is managed as love emerges in us over,
around, and through the shards of our broken beings. God's investment of love in us is hygienic when it comes to sin. Pure love is our
sole source of managing sin.

While Aristotle believed that the virtues came through a persistent effort of self-awareness and self-improvement, Paul directs us to a God of love who lives within those who seek and trust Him. Now, don't get me wrong. We are not passive in this process of managing sin. In the final chapter of this book, I will tackle that somewhat in depth. But for now, suffice it to say that we must desire to have our sins forgiven, our hearts changed, our minds renewed, our behavior transformed, our life a reflection of Jesus Christ. We cannot say yes to the fruit of the Spirit without saying no to the uncontrolled, unbridled rein of sin in our personal lives. But the fact is that God gives us a gift of desiring to be well and gives us the power to choose, when once we were without desire and prisoner to our baser instincts, living, it would seem, without choices. So, don't write off hard work, zeal, and patience if you want to play the wholeness game. Sin is serious business, and God's love is serious power, available to you and me.

Thinking of sins, or vices, by category, seeing how they affect us, and strategizing to live beyond at least some of the damaging effects of various types of sins does have value. And that's why I don't want to write Aristotle off. His thoughts and wisdom are valuable. One of the early church fathers tells us that all truth is God's truth. So, the universal realities of sin and virtue are very real, and are there for observation by all those who wish to observe. Aristotle is one such person. He was a moral luminary in many ways. He believed in the good life, well lived. He believed in truth telling and in so many other great moral values. The power of thinking in categories of sin and virtue is this: The categories become a microscope to help us in the process of self-awareness. Further, each category has the power to appeal to some people over the others.

I'd like to take a little space in this book to compare and differentiate the thinking of Paul and Aristotle as I understand it. There are definite parallels between Aristotle's seven virtues and Paul's eight manifestations of the fruit of the Spirit. Both lists share either identical words for virtue or contain words which, though different, come from the same linguistic field of meaning. In other words, though they are not exactly identical words and meanings they are synonymous with each other. For example, I can say something is cool and mean low temperature, or I can say chilled and mean low temperature. I can also say cool and popular. The two words are very different and are derived from two different sources, but they are synonymous in meaning. Perhaps calling these words closely approximate is most correct. Aristotle's list of virtues is closely approximate to Paul's fruit of the Spirit. I will speculate on specific correlations in each subsequent chapter of this book.

Both Paul and Aristotle regard gentleness as a core virtue. They use the same word to describe this trait of being well mannered in regard to attitudes and actions regarding other persons. Aristotle and Paul also share the word self-control. For Aristotle it is the virtue that controls lust. It's first on his list of seven virtues. Paul seems to use self-control as a blanket virtue that applies to the battle we wage against gluttony and lust. Paul places self-control eighth and last on his list.

I don't know for sure if we can make an iron-clad case for why both of these great thinkers placed their hierarchies of virtue precisely in their present order. We do know that Gregory the Great, who finalized the list of the Seven Deadly Sins, ranked each of the sins in terms of vileness and insidiousness. So, you will notice that Gregory regarded as most vile those sins which are internal and easily masked or denied.

If Paul's list of positive traits is headlined Love, Aristotle's is headlined Virtuous Living. Both lists embody similar thought. Inner issues pertaining to the well-being of the person prevail nearer the top in Paul's list. This is the main place where it differs from Aristotle, for whom social sins seem more important. But even more significant is Paul's view that God works something deep in us and then works it out. He believes that the Spirit of God opens a new attitude in us. The new attitude is an openness to a new experience of self and a new experience of God. Joy and peace, therefore, are paramount to Paul. What we see on the whole is a constellation of virtues that hold sin at bay.

While Paul and Aristotle reflect lists of virtues that are very parallel, their differences in priority show. And their understanding of the sources and resources for attaining virtues were likely quite different. For Aristotle, *eudaimonia* is defined as sublime happiness or "the good life." The word eudaimonia translates into English as "happiness," but given the way we tend to interpret happiness in Western civilization, it doesn't do justice to Aristotle's idea. So, referring to the "good life" or the "life well lived" is a better way to go. Aristotle's notion of the good life embodied attributes similar to peace and joy. At the same time, while Paul didn't include sobriety and liberality in the fruit of the Spirit, he did indeed encourage moderation in consumption and giving to God out of gratitude for God's grace in one's life.

When you take a little time to consider these two lists, it becomes clear that two great thinkers, separated by about three and a half centuries, were following a similar track. That convinces me that God introduced these ideas about virtue through the revealing presence of the Holy Spirit and from the contemplation of nature and the way things are.

So, the fruit of the Spirit is love, and God is in the process of shaping us by the power and presence of the Holy Spirit in the deepest part of our lives—in our essence. While Aristotle motivated others to be better people, Paul invites us to become intimate with a God who has the power and the loving desire to rebuild our lives from the inside out.

Little is said these days about character development. We talk about moral development in our schools and in our military academies. The concept of moral development is that we teach persons virtuous behavior by creating the correct climate, high expectations, and repetitive drills. Military academies are famous for instilling important values and morals such as loyalty. They also teach "Don't lie," "Don't cheat," "Don't steal."

But, all too often we fail to look at the source of our actions, which is our character. We won't make good progress on life's pilgrimage if we live from the outside in, trying to act and look as if we are virtuous. This sort of moral bootstrapping that is often lauded in reference to Ben Franklin's disciplines exacts a toll from most of us that we cannot pay. And, when we fail, we feel so discouraged, we just want to give up. Instead, I feel that real progress comes when we own our true current condition and allow God to take us where we need to go. Character forms slowly. But it's worth the wait. When God shapes character traits like self-control or kindness over the course of a lifetime, our lives make a difference.

The little things we do that demonstrate "kindness" serve to shape a kind character trait within us. The things we think and meditate upon as "kindness" further mold our attitudes and world-views. Kind people witness a war with horror. Even if the war is just, a kind person prays for peace and protection for the innocents. Unkind people say, "They've gone too far and now they'll pay as military forces crush them." Just as kind thoughts can shape a character trait of kindness, unkind thoughts and actions can serve to make brutes of us.

Somebody once said, "Character is who you are and what you do when no one is watching." I like this definition. As we consider sin and its consequences, we aren't doing so in order to win some sort of Righteousness Contest among our friends and neighbors. Rather, we are developing our character and seeking to possess an integrity that imparts life to self and others. We eschew behavior patterns that damage life and rob others.

Deep in our hearts, most of us truly long to be virtuous people; it's just that we have developed a character and a set of behavior patterns that make virtuous discipleship difficult to attain. The Apostle Paul was quick to admit this problem to himself, God, and his followers. Yet, inspired by the Spirit he speaks the Word of God.

His praises of virtue ring with hymnic beauty . . . "the fruit of the Spirit is love—which expresses itself as joy, peace, patience, kindness, goodness, faithfulness, gentleness, and self-control. Against such virtues, there is no law" (Galatians 5:22—Rowland paraphrase). What Paul is doing is extolling the virtue that awaits all who will imbibe. The last part of this biblical quote is of special interest: "Against such virtues, there is no law."

Think about it. There are laws against public drunkenness, assault laws against applied rage, antidiscrimination laws against some forms of small-mindedness. Yet there's no law against love. Who is going to arrest you for being too patient? When were you last indicted for gentleness? "I have had it with your kindness . . . abuse me!" is a phrase we are unlikely to hear.

We desire to live virtuous lives. All of us want to be known by the virtues we express in our lives. We deeply desire to do upright things against which no law can be written. The fruit of the Spirit can appear in the strangest places.

One particular Sunday morning several autumns ago, I stepped outside of the building where our church meets for a breath of fresh air after delivering my weekly sermon. We had some special guests in worship on this crisp, sunny morning. Two fellows who were addicted street people stood against a wall. They were clearly inebriated. They were telling me about their lives. What happened in those moments we visited is hard to explain. But, that's when my heart was softened and changed forever.

One of the men with whom I was visiting pointed to the other. He introduced his partner by saying, "This is our protector. He takes care of us all."

I responded by saying, "That's great" and I reached out to shake his hand.

The protector reached into his pocket and pulled out a terribly beat-up Bible with the flimsiest of pages and, for me, print too small to read. He said, "I love Jesus. I try to do what Jesus would do with people. I know I am bad for being a drunk. But I love Jesus and I am going to be with Him in heaven someday."

As I listened to the protector's own story and comments from his friend, I heard about a loving man who conducted conversations wherein he expressed a sincere interest in other people. As I spent a few moments in his presence, I understood what his friend was saying.

In the midst of a lifestyle of addiction, poor hygiene, theft, drug use, violence, and an almost total loss of self-control, here was a precious child of God trying to express virtues against which there is no law. His virtue was muffled by the decay of sin that had ripped him for years, but it was still there.

When we admit that there is a deep inner longing in all of us to become people whose character radiates virtue, we confess our greatest hope, our biggest dreams, the essence of our longings. So often we fear virtue because it seems so unattainable. Other times we fear it because of how concepts of virtue have been twisted.

Christians are often thought of as negative moralists. Paul is often accused of being ungracious. But what Paul really means to do, if we read his words correctly, is to get us to acknowledge the reality of sin and move beyond it to live in the virtues which God created as gifts to the human race, and which God empowers within us by the function of the Spirit. Any contemplation of one's sin problem, as grotesque and painful as it may be, is a simultaneous invitation to a quality of divine grace that brings the joy, simplicity, and peace of virtue. We are designed for beautiful lives such as these.

Aristotle was joined by Paul as a great shaper in the virtue-and-vice dialogue. Both figures contributed greatly to the thinking of early church fathers and mothers.

While Aristotle's polarity was based upon the difference between virtue and vice, Gregory's polarity is between the fruit of the Spirit and sin. Aristotle, Paul, and Gregory were not far apart. That which Christians now call sin was referred to by Aristotle as "sources of blame," or vices. Just as Paul articulated that there is no law against love, no legislation against the fruit of the Spirit, Aristotle believed that there was no end to the positive power of the virtuous, so much so that virtue in practice rendered a person blameless. Falling short of being blameless (exercising vices) resulted in behaviors Aristotle called "sources of blame." The positive character attributes of the virtues were reckoned by Aristotle as "sources of praise."

Gregory and Paul, the two Christian thinkers, take a somewhat opposite approach to that of Aristotle. In our study, we will see that Gregory begins with the problem of sin. His list of virtues was not at all dissimilar to Aristotle's, but he felt the need to come to grips, first and foremost, with the blocks to virtue. Only when these obstacles were encountered and removed (or partially removed) could one move forward.

In the writings of Christian spiritual masters, one never gets a strong sense of accomplishment in the battle against sin, but rather a new level of enlightenment, a heightened desire to be right with God and an abiding hope that a little progress can be made each day along the way. As we consider the Seven Deadly Sins and you see yourself as the "poster person" for one or more of them, please don't despair. There is hope, and that's the real reason I am writing this book.

At this point, a brief overview of the Seven Deadly Sins will be helpful. We will revisit each of these constellations of human error at length in the chapters that follow.

Looking at ourselves through the lens of these seven areas of sin is a daunting task, full of emotional terror.

It's no wonder sin is not a popular topic. But it is a popular character trait. We are all broken. We all sin. What will happen if we accept our dark side and work with it, rather than deny it? What if we realize, like Jakob Dylan of the band The Wallflowers, that ". . . the same black line that was drawn on you was drawn on me." We are all marked by sin.

The human condition is a regular heartache for the Creator who desires to live in communion with, not separation from, His Creation. It's also a heartache with which we must live. Together. We are in it together. In fact, we might even be able to manage it better together than alone. The same black line of sin runs through each of us. And as we discovered earlier there is no getting around the reality of sin for any living human being.

We would all like to rise up to meet the nemesis of sin in our lives. The question is "How?" And, of course, the response is not an easy two-step formula. Rather, the answer is found in active spirituality that nurtures all that is good in humanity. Developing virtue also means accepting bad, in the sense that we stop glossing over and justifying our own sin. Now another temptation we must avoid is realizing the gravity of sin and then throwing our hands in the air and giving up. This is actually a temptation toward sloth, which is itself one of the deadly sins.

If you have followed the four Star Wars movies, you know that there is a mystical "Force" that can be harnessed for good. But, the Force can also be accessed for evil. The sages and heroes depicted in George Lucas's movies work to keep from going over to "the dark side." Well, that's not a bad analogy for us on our spiritual journeys. We are setting a direction in this world amid many powerful forces, and we all want to use those forces for good. We don't want to go over to the dark side.

About the time I graduated high school, a watershed book hit the market. Its concept of "I'm okay, you're okay" has greatly affected our society in which people are attempting to become noble, mature, and good human beings. But I find a deep flaw in the very title of this book. It assumes that we are good and that exploring our human goodness discovers our virtue. You can observe this approach on many daytime television shows and radio talk shows that laud personal growth and human understanding. The optimism in the possibility of humans fixing themselves denies both the reality of God and the gravity of sin.

As I survey the Holocaust, and more recently Bosnia, Rwanda, and other international travesties, I just don't think the premise of human beings being good holds up. Rather, I think my preferred title to this human development concept would be "I'm not okay, you're not okay, but that's okay."

I cannot truly seek to "grow" and "become" until I really come to grips with what holds me back from the mature goodness and virtue that I desire. I am becoming a better golfer. I enjoy golf. But I didn't begin improving until I faced the fact that I had a wild, almost spastic swing that did nothing but hit balls a long and impressive way in the wrong direction. My first golf lessons were a severe discipline. Nothing about a good golf swing felt native or good to me. But, several years and thirty strokes better in my golf game score, I am realizing there is a better way to golf and it is certainly more fulfilling.

Such is life. There is a better way. Our seven deadly proclivities actually guide us toward the light of a new way of living . . . and those same deadly sins place us in solidarity with all human beings, so that we no longer fool ourselves by trying to "put ourselves up" while we play the "put down" game of judgmentalism with those around us.

Our first response must be to pray for the desire to be virtuous. *Sins We Love* is all about seven categories of distorted behavior and attitudes that are so synonymous with our nature that we actually love them. Face it, we all chuckle as we make jokes about our envy of someone or our appetite for material things. While we are still in the process of trying to discover virtue, we normalize our vices by doing comedy routines about them. Now, I don't think this is all bad, because if we laugh at ourselves, we just might find it a little bit less painful to accept our need for change.

Before we move on, let me defend myself for just a moment. I am anything but a legalist, a moralist, or an old-fashioned thinker. I listen to lots of contemporary music, catch most of the movies released each year, read novels, and love watching *The Simpsons* and *The X-Files*. At no time in reading this book should you consider me a bastion of moral strength. Far from it, I fail daily. But what I find as years go by is that I am more and more motivated by love for God and love for others to become a virtuous person.

The kind of character development that I am articulating in this book is a long, slow process. It takes a lifetime of reflection, conversation, and action to bear fruit. There is no end to the learning. It is highly personal and deeply internal. It is core stuff.

I have come to realize in my spiritual journey through life that inner change is the hardest and most threatening form of change. We feel so vulnerable. We are often motivated by things such as guilt and shame, which cannot take us where we want and need to go.

Guilt is a bad motivator. It's the messenger inside us that says, "You did a bad thing." A quick adjustment in course and we convince ourselves that we are okay again. No permanent change. Plus, one cannot build a virtue on a negative assertion such as "I will not be unkind." Instead, we must proceed from the basis of "This is what it means to be kind. . . ."

Shame is the menace that tells us that we are bad . . . that we are flawed beyond repair. Such an assertion can throw us into a major funk. We become inactive because it seems that nothing we do could make any difference in our lives or our world as long as we are still a part of things. Shame destroys our soul in a sort of emotional/spiritual suicide. We see ourselves as unredeemable when shame takes over. To be honest, no action motivated by shame will result in anything less than a spectacular display of one of the Seven Deadly Sins.

I was visiting with a sociologist who works with runaway kids involved in prostitution. The expert told me that nearly all of these children were abused sexually as youngsters. The acted-upon lust of some family member or friend left a residue of worthlessness. Shame then made these teens numb to any healthy consideration of what it means to be a sexual being. In the end, sex becomes a shame-motivated vocation of prostitution—accompanied by a life of incredible risk, danger, and despair.

Guilt and shame are not the proper tools to use in the midst of our conviction of sin. When we know we have sinned, what we need is love. Love is the greatest power of all. Nothing can conquer love. Love is absolute spiritual and moral rocket fuel.

When we practice self-examination, we should not do so out of dread, or with a desire to punish ourselves with guilt and shame. Instead, we should do self-examination out of love.

Most women I know practice breast self-examination to check for breast cancer. They don't do this because they ought to, or to find a way to condemn themselves. They do it out of a healthy sense of belovedness. They love themselves and their own lives and they want to remain healthy and alive to love the ones who love them.

When a woman finds a lump in a self-examination, she doesn't condemn herself, she goes for advice and medical treatment if necessary.

The self-examination of our hearts for sin is a very similar process and it's all about love. Love of God, love of self, and love of others. I love God and want to be intimately connected with my Creator. I love myself and want to be all that I can be. I love my family and friends and neighbors and want to live in a way that nurtures others. Love is a motivation that cannot be suppressed. Love is patient. Love is persistent. Love believes. Love hopes. Love overlooks wrongs done by others. Love never fails.

Welcome to an exhibit of human nature and a glimpse of glory all stirred together. We begin with the sin of Pride.

THREE

Proud of Being
Proud: PRIDE

Pride exists in many forms. Sometimes it is even expressed in humor and taken lightheartedly. A Midwestern university known for its high academic standards and historically low football achievements has led the student section to be quite creative in their support of a usually hapless football team. They have developed a cheer to the tune of "We Will Rock You" by the band Queen, that goes, "We Will, We Will, Hire You." In addition they have placards that they carry outside the stadium after a game and parade around the visiting team's bus. The placards read, "You may have beaten us today, but tomorrow, you work for me."

Frankly, I found these behaviors a cute way to cope with a losing football tradition. I believe the intention of the students is simply fun loving. Yet, the student section's response to their opponent carries an edge of arrogance that is at the heart of pride. In Latin, the word for pride is *superbia*. It means "above" or "better." One English dictionary defines pride as "an immoderate degree of self-esteem or an overvaluation set upon persons by themselves, which undervalues and oppresses others." Pride is a sin of too much love for the self. It's a twisted, polluted form of love. Love diminished by the nature of its object, the self. I am not accusing a Big Ten school's student cheer of being pride in itself, but it amusingly models that "I am better than you" aspect of pride. We use pride to elevate ourselves. Some of us think that we are cut of a better cloth. We feel that we don't struggle with the things that seem to sink other people like lack of self-discipline, inability to manage finances, failed relationships, or mental health issues. We develop our list of what is right and what is wrong with human beings. And as we look down our nose at others, our pride places us on the achievement list of all that is right, while at the same time condemning those around us to a life on the side of all that is wrong.

Pride, according to many theologians and ethicists, is the true issue in the human condition we know as sinfulness. Pride is the exaltation of self. It's so subtle how pride works. I'll use myself as an example. I am a strong personality. I am pretty tough. Therefore, it is very tempting for me to look down my nose at anyone who is not dominant and not tough and persevering. My own gifts, which God has given me to live my destiny in this world, become my enemy. My gifts are elevated as the universal standard to which all must attain. My gifts get twisted into being my pride and, therefore, being my enemy. A study in organizational development showed that one of the main causes of failure and/or ineffectiveness in business organizations is too many people of the same disposition and gifts. Pride beckons us to welcome all those who are just like us and look down our nose at the uniqueness of others. Corporate pride can kill a company, or a society.

Sometimes pride exalts our strengths. Sometimes it covers our insecurities and weaknesses. I once saw a bumper sticker that read, "I'm fat. You're ugly. At least I can diet." Cute, yes. An attempt to cover a struggle with an assertion of superiority, yes.

Not all varieties of pride are bad. In fact, I am convinced that some forms are good. I am also convinced that we frequently misuse the word in English. We use the word pride to stand for "dignity" and "integrity" quite often. When we say, "Don't you have any pride in yourself?" We are not asking people to launch into a manic episode of *superbia*. Instead, we are saying, "Your life matters, so express a little dignity."

When we think of the pride of Gandhi, Martin Luther King, Jr., Mother Teresa, or Albert Einstein, we think of the dignity and integrity of those people. Gandhi once said, "My life is my message." These people were so "integrated," or "put together," that there was a consistency in what they thought, felt, said, and did. Wow. We don't want to downgrade this definition of pride, especially since it has been so redemptive in our human societies. As for me, I would rather drop the word pride and call it integrity or dignity. We all want people to value themselves. Goodness, if sociologists and social psychologists are correct, there is probably no greater source of trouble in our society than the endemic plague of low self-esteem and undeveloped self-identity. So, let's be wise in not condemning good self-esteem and integrity. But we must also be wise enough not to allow integrity and good self-esteem to become sources of pride. Pride is a sin we love because it grows up like a life-choking weed in the midst of a beautiful garden that is our soul.

Pride in its more destructive form is at the heart of all human sin. Pride is the assertion of self above all authority, all space, and all time. To declare oneself "superb" or better or above is the first step toward building a life that dismantles the soul and poisons all of Creation. It's really difficult to keep a world in balance when over 5 billion people stake a claim as "god." The ascent to godlike status, the placement of absolute authority in the self, is the end state of pride, and the end of civilization.

Pride hits all of us. It's part of our human condition. Rather than argue about who is most prideful and how prideful I am, as if we could measure it, I am committed to a course of awareness. I cannot attend to a problem that I don't recognize and acknowledge.

Think of this in medical terms. You have a sore shoulder. It's not so bad that you have to do anything with it. You figure, "Boy, I must be sleeping on it wrong." You work around it and ignore it until the pain is too great. Finally, you go to your physician, who tells you that you have a problem with your rotator cuff muscles. Now, your unidentified and increasingly intense ache has a name. That's awareness. This is a great first step.

But the first step of recognition is not enough. A proper response is required. Diagnosing something is of no value if you don't treat the problem as fully as possible. Pride is a good place to start the practice of diagnosing and taking action. Pride is so universal; we all find our little ways to play God.

Yes, I said to play God. The exercise of *superbia* is to claim the role of God. Pride says, "I am better and of higher authority than any other force." Many religious people have distorted the concept of God. Some view God as some sort of Cosmic Twinkie who watches Creation ambivalently, and benignly. Others view God as this angry maniac who is anxious to wreak havoc and judgment upon anyone who doesn't live up to His demanding standards. A more orthodox and historical view of God is that the Creator and Sustainer of life is all-loving, all-knowing, all-powerful, and always present. This is a God who is "for us."

Pride places "me" in the center of life, when the Lord and Giver of life, God, should be at the center. Why in the world would I want to oust a God who is personal, loving, powerful, and my constant companion? I don't think you or I would attempt to supplant such a God, who is simply not supplantable. But something inside of us that we are learning to identify as pride cajoles us into making statements, nurturing thoughts, and demonstrating behaviors contrary to a belief in the sovereignty of God.

When it comes to pride and the exaltation of self, the misunderstanding of God could be a significant contributor to the problem. I think we would do best to look at God's role in the universe and make a mental note to ourselves that says, "Job taken. No need to apply." While we might be disappointed that the opportunity to become God is not available to us, it is also quite a source of encouragement and hope to know that God is not mad at us. In fact, God pities our broken state and desires to help us toward wholeness. In classic Christian theology God is viewed as the Creator, Sustainer, and Redeemer. God does it all, and does it all well. He makes it; He keeps it going; He fixes it when it's broken. This is a God worthy of our trust. God is the source of our redemption. We hand God our sin and God hands us forgiveness, a new perspective, and the power to become whole.

If God is all-loving, all-powerful, and always present, why would any living creature wish to rule God out of the mix of life? The answer is mind-boggling, but simple. We just don't like the competition. So, we buy into a spiritual error that says, "I'll decide what God is and what God says." At the point I assert myself as master of my ship, I attempt to displace God from His rightful place in my life.

One of my childhood friends had a little sister. All of us who were big brothers or big sisters know our shortcomings as siblings, but the universal gripe about younger brothers and sisters is that they won't leave older brothers or sisters alone when they have friends over. In fact, they often become obnoxious. My friend's little sister had elevated obnoxiousness to a world-class level. Every once in a while, my buddy would boil over at her tagging along and smart-mouthing and go after her. As he angrily approached, the little sister would cover her eyes and say, "I can't see you, so you can't see me." For a moment, she had a nice fantasy, and then came the reality of life in the form of a pummeling. Through the years I have thought many times about this young girl and her antics, because her behavior is so close to what many of us do with God. "I can't see you, so you can't see me." This effort to truly block God out is about as successful as my friend's sister was in hiding, but we do it anyway.

One of the sad moments in the Christian story takes place in the garden of Eden. Our foreparents, Adam and Eve, have sinned against God and now have hunkered down in a secure place in the garden. God comes looking for the first family. He knows right where they are. They are helplessly trying to avoid a God who doesn't miss a thing. When confronted, they display their inability to make a good argument by saying they cannot come to God because they are naked. When finally confronted the two humans try to blame each other for their sin.

This ancient story teaches us a lot about sin, especially the sin of pride. First, it tells us that God doesn't miss a thing. God's in charge. Second, God is passionate to be in a relationship with human beings. Third, humans pretend to hide from God. Fourth, humans are ashamed of things (such as nakedness) that they ought not to be ashamed of. Fifth, human beings are not ashamed of what they ought to be ashamed of (openly disobeying God). Sixth, human beings have very little self-awareness. Seventh, humans always have someone else to blame when they are in the wrong. They don't like to take responsibility for their choices.

Pride is unleashed in all the actions we take to replace or block out God. And if there are several major aspects to the ascent of pride, the summit becomes the inability to be wrong.

Some thinkers, including popular Christian psychiatrist M. Scott Peck, say that the root of all evil is the need to be right. Self-justification kills. Pride blocks us from the wisdom and authority God should have in overseeing our lives. We become our own judge and jury. And we will allow our pride to do just about anything it wants with us. In other words, pride becomes a runaway train. Our sense of superiority and completeness runs loose. Pride begets pride and soon we have fully invested ourselves into thinking we are what the world is all about.

I know of a man and woman whose marriage split some time ago. The woman left the man over his use of pornographic materials. She considered it an offense against her, God, and even her husband's personal wholeness.

During the separation between this man and woman, the woman was overcome by sorrow at the thought of packing in her relationship. She was inspired to believe that they could work things out.

She came to me and I recommended counseling. She was all for it. Her husband refused.

The husband said his wife overreacted to his doing a very "normal" male thing. "I am not about to go to counseling. There's nothing wrong with our marriage." He had done nothing wrong. If she knew what was right for her she'd just come home and knock off all the fussing. I was unable to convince him that he had any responsibility in their marriage problems. He was a successful businessman with money, power, and excellent health. He didn't need God, even though he attended church regularly. He didn't need forgiveness or redirecting because he was never wrong. He thought he was healthy and whole, which is the lie of pride. The displacement of God and the overassertion of the self that comes with pride places the prideful in a constant state of self-adoration. This worship of the self is often masked by noble titles like "self-made man." Believe me, there is no such thing as a self-made man or self-made woman. We are all God-made.

Pride presses heavily into our interactions with others. Once we have removed God from the mix, we presume to lord it over other humans. This is the juncture where callous rejection of God and a condescending attitude toward others emerge as full-blown pride. I once heard it said that those who continually look down never look up to see God. They also look down upon others rather than seeing them eye to eye.

One might say, "I know it seems like I am looking down upon others, but in truth, I do believe that I am superior in some significant ways." While it is true that most of us are better than many others in some area of personal giftedness, it is not correct to say that anyone is better than everyone in every way. But this error of being fully superior is the intellectual flaw.

One of the joys and sorrows of being a pastor is the tremendous amount of time that a pastor gets to spend with people. It's a joy to see a spiritually hungry or hurting person takes steps to become whole. It's a sorrow to deal with people who are prideful. I have a dear friend who thinks she is morally, socially, intellectually, and physically superior to everyone else. The poor soul is pathetic. She is constantly alienating others and then writing them off. During one particular meeting about some leadership issues in the church, she offered a blanket condemnation of all the church's elders, "They just don't get it. I don't know how they get by."

For this friend, even speed limits are for old people who aren't as coordinated as she is. She arrogantly told me, "People over the age of sixty shouldn't be allowed to drive and there should be no speed limits." When I told her that I wouldn't like to drive on highways with no speed limits having tried just that in Germany, she responded, "Well, if you cannot drive really, really well, use public transportation."

My friend is terribly tormented. Everyone around her appears to be an idiot. No one quite knows how to cook, clean, recycle garbage, and keep house like she does. Nobody is smart enough to understand her complex social concerns and political insights. On the whole, the only company she isn't bored with is her own. And she's getting more and more time on her own as her list of friends dwindles daily. When I first met her, I knew she was very smart— and she seemed discerning. But what seemed discerning turned out to be critical and faultfinding. The person I have come to know in subsequent years is a person with an unrestrained case of pride that will lead to her destruction.

Many of us sense that we are in this world for a reason. We know that we have been created with special gifts and abilities. That's true. Each of us is a unique, unrepeatable miracle from God. And to live life at its fullest, we must discover our gifts and abilities and use them to the fullest. Unfortunately many of us have been broken or wounded along the way by family, friends, schools, and perhaps churches. These social injuries ravage our self-esteem. We begin to talk to ourselves saying, "I am a nothing. I'm not good at anything. No one cares if I live or die."

Such negative statements wear down spirit, soul, and psyche. We can't live with ourselves in such a negative state, so we begin to compensate. "Well, I may be a no good so and so, but at least I'm better than Alex over there. He's never made partner at the firm and he's fifty."

So, in an attempt to "be somebody," you and I very easily usher pride into the arena of life. We clearly mark where we are "better" and carefully boundary ourselves not to hear where we are "worse." Then we dig in, creating a personal myth of superiority that we somehow feel will give us a reason to live.

I do not consider myself to be antitherapeutic. I see much need for highly skilled and passionate people-helpers in fields ranging from psychiatry to training programs and I have seen the healing re-sults of therapy. But I must also critique the therapeutic movement. Too many times I have seen people who are very troubled go into a client-centered therapist's office and come out rationalizing their pathology with some counselor's seal of approval on it. We must be careful of how we deal with the self.

Pride is a well-disguised and dangerous adversary. We think we are gaining confidence and moving toward health and integrity and wholeness, but in reality we are developing a well-honed system for the delivery and protection of aggressive self-centeredness and nonaccountable, radical individualism.

There is a third flaw contributing to pride, this one an emotional flaw. It is the voice inside that says, "Mine. Mine. Mine." It's a voice that spoke loudly as a child, was met with great disapproval on numerous occasions and suppressed. But in our desire to rule not just our own world, but also the entire universe, we seek to increase our sphere of influence and learn new ways of saying, "mine" by reading books on negotiation and assertiveness training. Now "mine" is couched in language about my wants and needs, rights and sensitivities. We know what we have coming to us, and doggone it, we're going to get it.

The name for this emotional flaw is entitlement. The world owes us something. Go out and get what's yours. The best revenge is to live well. So, we stake a claim about what we deserve, and we use every tool available to us to demand our due. The entitlement mindset is a huge concern in our modern society. We feel the world owes us everything. In entitlement, we replace dreams, goals, and opportunities with expectations. We expect the world, and every creature in it, to bow to us, to come at our bidding, and to give us what we want for the purpose of making us happy.

Entitlement attitudes expect governments, families, friends, churches, workplaces, to cater to our every need. The interesting thing about entitlement is that it is a paralyzing form of pride. By paralyzing I mean that our superiority claim becomes so emphatic that we actually abdicate the dignity of taking responsibility for our lives and our choices. In the paralysis of entitlement, we stop our process of becoming and we place our happiness squarely on the shoulders of anyone we can find. In addition, when we are not happy with our lot in life, paralyzing pride allows us to blame others for their failure to take care of us and please us. The blaming language of entitlement thinking is a huge blustering front that distracts us from what's really wrong—ourselves.

Of course, once we have declared ourselves superior, we also have a keen recognition that we deserve more than anyone else. Then, when we don't get everything we think we have coming, we exalt ourselves to an even higher level and make bold claims of our achievements and our superiority. No one is quite as smart as we are. No one is quite as hard working. No one handles people as well. No one understands God as well. The symptom of pride is that feeling we all know and love and hate simultaneously that tells us that we are special, that we are better than others. In pride, we hold God to his promises, pretending to be God ourselves, and in so doing step aside from an outpouring of love and mercy from God.

I worked in broadcasting for a number of years. I loved the daily challenge of being entertaining and informative. I met wonderful people and made great friends. And because radio involves artistic-type personalities, I met some truly interesting people. No one filled the bill of someone who grew pride into entitlement more than one young newsman whom we'll call Jimmy Olson.

Still in his early twenties, Jimmy would confidently swagger into the station staff meetings, joining broadcast veterans who had years of experience, some as much as twenty-five years on the job. These were people who knew their jobs, and a relative newcomer myself, I kept my mouth shut around them. Each time, Jimmy would take over the meeting, expounding his great knowledge, profound insights, and vast experience. And do you know where this wisdom was obtained? As a news writer at a college radio station in rural South Dakota. People around the broadcast house didn't buy his prideful airs. Other employees mercilessly teased him about it. At this point rather than say, "Okay, you've got me. I'm nailed. Lay off," Jimmy went to great lengths, even writing a paper, to extol the real-life virtues of working in campus radio. And this young man would look into the eyes of knowing veterans and sneer at them as if they were stupid. Some of those professionals I worked with are still in the business, some in Seattle, some in Chicago, Los Angeles, New York, and Cleveland. The entitled young man is considerably older now, but even today lasts little more than a year in any job—and he's running out of major markets in America in which to find a job.

Tragically, my young friend really did have some talent. He just felt that the broadcast industry owed him respect and a reputation that he had not come close to earning. And his sense of entitlement soured him. His prideful unwillingness to develop an accurate worldview and an accurate assessment of himself set him up to be a mockery among his peers, and a much less effective person in his career. When things didn't go the way he had them scripted, he became bitter. Rather than listening to those who were the best in the business on the air and saying, "I am going to give this my all, and who knows, someday, I may be a top broadcaster. If not, I will at least have tried my hardest." Instead, he was busy figuring out whom he was better than.

Wounded by his lack of progress and his strained relationships, my young friend's sense of pride swelled to a new magnitude. Psychologists and spiritual directors often note that people who become obsessively prideful actually begin foraging for knowledge. They learn little tidbits about this and that, thriving on gossip, so they can stake their rightful claim as the grand know-it-all.

I am sure that my problem with pride runs as deeply as anyone else's. I don't presume to have all of the answers on this matter. But I have developed a couple of tests that I apply to myself and others. My tests are fundamental examinations of people interactions. The first is that when I see someone in action, I ask, "How does he treat the people that he doesn't have to be nice to?" If the answer is positive, I am probably seeing someone with a tolerable level of pride. If the answer is "not very well," then there's a problem.

During my years as a sports broadcaster, I saw some really stupendous athletes. Our city was blessed to have one fellow who was truly spectacular. He seemed so humble and self-effacing, especially in front of the media. He knew all the right things to say to look "mom and apple pie." One day, while covering this fellow's team at a practice, I saw a young college intern come out of the locker room literally in tears. I knew him, so I went to chat. He told me that Mr. Superstar has been cussing him out, humiliating him in front of players and making him a laughingstock. He also told me that the star made him do demeaning jobs and carry his gear, and that he actually made a daily routine of throwing his sweaty undergarments in this poor intern's face.

After all, the young intern was just a faceless college kid. The star was, well, the star! He was better than some no-name intern. He had worked hard to become a pro and deserved the right to enslave and humiliate others. Mr. Star was getting his due at the expense of others.

Now, I would like to offer an additional test for each of us. It's another pride indicator. When you watch someone in action in a social setting, does she help others become bigger and stronger, or does she drain the life out of others to make herself big.

You see, our pride can be like a banyan tree. Nothing grows in its shade and its leaves poison the ground. Everything within the reach of a banyan tree dies and gives way to the banyan. How do we escape the inevitable gravity of pride? If Gregory the Great and other Christian thinkers were convinced that pride in some way is the root of every sin, how might we frail ones deal with such an adversary?

I believe that there is a helpful practice for keeping pride in check. Think of it as a sort of "moral flossing." Just as we floss our teeth daily to prevent tooth decay, so we must do some moral flossing as well. In the business of spirituality, these "flossing" behaviors are called disciplines—those activities that promote health and well-being. The discipline for managing pride is called humility.

Humility is a word derived from the Latin word *humus*, which means "of the earth." Humility keeps pride in check. To be of the earth means to be nothing more and nothing less than who and what we really are. Humility means owning up to our gifts and using them. Humility is accurate self-assessment and self-assertion. Humility prevents us from understating or overstating who we are. A proper sense of humility is derived from proximity to God. I once heard it said that humility is standing on our tiptoes next to God at God's full stature.

I teach preaching classes at a local seminary and was addressing a kind woman in my class with a life story that would make anyone cry: addictions, crime, family troubles, you name it. She was overly timid and protective of herself, when in fact she should have been more confident and bold.

She answered me by saying, "That's just really hard for me. I have trouble projecting myself as anyone special."

I said, "But you are special. Look at your story and what God can do through you. You have so much to offer. You are a fine communicator. Speak the truth that comes from God's word and your life with enthusiasm and confidence."

Here is a woman who has, with God's gracious help, gotten her life very together and become an ordained minister. During her time of preparation, when she preached in my class, she delivered brilliantly crafted sermons, tested by the fires of real life, in a timid, unconfident manner.

I finally had to take her aside and say, "You are gifted at this. One manifestation of pride is denying a true gift and guarding ourselves. Next time you get in that pulpit, let it rip." She did. And it was a joy to watch. Humility means owning who we are. While we own who we are, we must be careful not to overstate who we are. After all, "of the earth" means earthy, rooted, grounded, natural.

I was recently devastated by a friend telling me that he and his wife had left one of the couples' groups in our church because one of the members thought so much of himself. My friend said, "I feel rotten saying it, but my wife and I just can't stand to be around Bob any longer. He is an arrogant know-it-all who has no evidence in his life, his relationships, or his career to back up his claim of greatness."

There is a wonderful passage in the New Testament that speaks to this issue of humility. It comes from a letter written by the Apostle Paul to the people of Galatia. Let me paraphrase what it says:

"Let each person examine his or her own life and work. Don't be fascinated with yourself, and don't compare yourself to others. Instead do the very best you can with what you have, knowing that God is your audience."

Doesn't that bit of biblical wisdom ring of truth to you? I must spend my time looking at me, making a proper assessment of my gifts, my vocation, my weaknesses, and my failures. And it simply doesn't do any good to compare myself to any one person—only God. I am not in this world to impress other people with my greatness. I am in this world to please God.

The amazing thing is that when we work against our own best

self, keeping an eye on how God is shaping us, we give other people some room to grow. Humility (*humus*) becomes a sort of fertile ground for relationships where others flourish around us. Soon everyone is winning.

If humility is the practice for keeping pride in check, how do we put legs under it? Several thoughts:

Get used to the idea that there is a God. Get used to the idea that you are one of God's beloved creatures. God made you and you are special. These fundamental ideas about God root us in a self-esteem that guards against pride. My wife has a poster in her office. It says, "Fundamental truths of human enlightenment: 1. There is a God. 2. You are not God."

There are a number of ways to work this recognition that God is God and we're not. One is to pray. Thank God for the gift of your life. Thank God for creating the world. Thank God for your gifts. Thank God for the challenges in your life that are shaping you and keeping you on the growing edge. When you pray, literally say, "God, you are God and I am not. I open myself to you and your love. You are ruler of all nature. Speak into my life." One of the words often used in Scripture for worshiping God is to "magnify God"—it means just what it says. To magnify God means to focus on God to such a degree that the Ancient of Days fills our entire field of vision. In other words, praying ourselves into the meditation of God that accepts the reality of God's infinite and perfect attributes.

Another step toward recognizing God in our lives is to set aside a regular time for reading and wrestling with the content of the Old and New Testaments. The Bible is the Word of God and its words keep us mindful of God. If God is the master builder of the universe, the Bible is the blueprint.

Worship is also a good tool. Go to a vibrant church where songs of praise are directed at God. Practice extending the magnification of God that you have practiced in private prayer into the context of public worship with other believers. While we sing to God of His greatness, we also remind ourselves that we aren't God.

If you think God-recognition is a tough discipline, then you're really going to find this one hard. After all, it's easy to rationalize that God is superior. But it is very hard to rationalize keeping ourselves eye to eye with others rather than looking down.

The way we manage this is by realizing that the human condition is universal. We are all flawed. It doesn't really make sense to point out the flaws of others and count them as more serious than our own. Because in the end, we're all in the same position. We are all sinful. Comparing sins by their weight does little good. Our condition of sin is not treatable by our own resources. But pride leads us to believe that our sins are less egregious than those of our fellows.

There's an amusing but telling story about Sir Winston Churchill being quite inebriated at a party during World War II. Apparently, a woman despairing of his loud, abrasive behavior came up to him and said, "Sir Churchill, you are drunk." To which he responded, "Yes, I am drunk, and you, madam, are ugly. But tomorrow I shall be sober, and you will still be ugly."

If we were to honestly admit it, most of us are like Winston; held accountable internally or externally, we are quite prone to try and vindicate ourselves as "flawed" yet "better."

In the eighties a well-known televangelist, Jim Bakker, was overtaken by a sexual scandal. He was the center of controversy. Another familiar televangelist from the South immediately came on TV denouncing the man's sexual sin and calling for him to leave the public ministry. The Southern preacher said that this must be done, "to keep the righteousness and purity of the church." Several months later, the one who knew "exactly how to handle this sort of thing" was caught in a motel with a prostitute. His fall was greater than the first man's.

Bottom line: We're all a bit of a mess. We do much better if we deal gently with one another's weaknesses, and are careful about our own claims to greatness. In Galatians, Paul tells us that if we catch someone in sin, we ought to restore him to wholeness gently and be very careful that we do not fall prey to the deceitfulness of sin in our own lives. This is good advice.

When I hear of a politician getting in trouble with shady financial deals or becoming the star of a sex scandal, I have to say to myself, "It's not that hard to do. I could do this. A few crazy thoughts on an off day . . . and I'm right there with him."

I must identify and think through my solidarity with other human beings to avoid the sin of pride. And, I must learn to pity the weaknesses of others as surely as I pity my own.

There is a particular fruit of the Spirit which nurtures humility within us. It is called kindness. To be kind means to be warm, considerate, generous, to speak well of another. Kindness also involves patience and generosity. My summation of kindness evokes a fairness from us in which we desire to treat others the way we want to be treated. It also puts people all on the same level irrespective of lifestyle, gender, race, or ethnicity. Kindness embraces the solidarity of the human race. Kindness sees each person as potential-laden but sin-flawed. One of the ways we sharpen our understanding of humility in action is stretching ourselves into some random acts of kindness. Aristotle's virtue word that parallels Paul's use of kindness is righteousness. Righteousness has to do with "doing right" by others. It has a justice component. When we see that we are flawed, sinful, broken people, we do right by others when we accept their limitations as we would our own.

Humility also means treating life as a gift and taking full advantage of all that we have, rather than the clamoring, restless scavenging we do to get all we think we deserve. Humility says, "I am who I am. I am who I am becoming. I have all I need to get where I need to go."

Letting go of what we haven't got and embracing what we have is the secret of life. Being fully alive today is being a faithful steward of what's within our reach. Anything else leads us to living an illusion.

I used to think time and again that I deserved better pay in my jobs. I would constantly chafe at the amount I was paid and assert that I was worth more. The problem was, even when I did get raises, they didn't come as gifts, or even as perks for working hard and accomplishing goals. Instead, they came as morsels representing less than I thought I was worth.

When I finally let go of entitlement thinking, I began to say to myself, "This is where I am this year. I don't know where I will be next year, but one thing is for sure . . . I am going to make something of the three hundred sixty-five days between now and then."

Our discussion of pride has led us down numerous paths, each one valuable. If you are reading this book and integrating ideas about the issue of sin, you will probably notice that pride rears a bit of its head in each of the other six deadly sins. We would like to say we hate sin, but it is so ingrained in us that it feels quite natural. No sin exemplifies this ingrained nature more than pride. Pride is truly at the heart of all the sins we love.

FOUR

I Want What I Haven't Got: ENVY

Have you ever outright wanted to be someone else? To be who that person is and possess what he or she has? Have you felt that feeling that is described in the world of colors as green? Green with envy.

Most of my adult life has been spent in front of people: radio, television, video, film, as a professor and as a preacher. But my secret dream is to be a rock-and-roll star—a guitar virtuoso with a passionate and powerful voice like Bono of the band U2.

Well, it just so happens that the lead guitarist in our church band, Jeff, is pretty much a virtuoso. He plays with incredible touch and sensitivity, but he can also be extremely powerful. I see him radiate sharing his gifts and I sense God's pleasure in seeing this precious creature of His make a six-stringed instrument spout such a variety of sound for worship and special music.

I should probably respond to all of this by saying, "Wow! God has really blessed you and watching you play makes my heart soar." But I couldn't say that in total honesty many days. You see, I want his gifts. I admire Jeff to the point of envy. It can actually be distracting to me. It causes me to lose sight of my own gifts and calling and I wind up fantasizing about something that I could never attain. Give me eight hours a day of guitar lessons and singing practice for three years with all the best teachers and technology and I still couldn't lead "Pass It On" properly.

That's what envy does. It gets us looking down our noses at ourselves and peering over our neighbor's fence wanting what he or she has. Wanting what you haven't got does not lead to a peaceful, joy-filled life.

While pride is a disguisable and easily rationalized sin, envy is a hidden sin. Most of the time we don't want to tell anyone but our smoldering inner self what we're really thinking.

In a recent film about several single adults living in a large city who were all looking for serious life partners, two women in this friendship group were preparing a meal together, and as they did, one of them mentioned that one of their male friends had a new steady girlfriend. The other woman inquired, "What's she like?" The answer was, "Long legs, skinny, beautiful face, and dark hair— you know, a regular nightmare."

No doubt most of us find the interaction from a popular movie amusing. But it is a modern-day example of envy. What isn't cute about it is the way envy causes us to change the way we think about ourselves and others. It is not amusing to see envy drain the life energy right out of its victims. When we begin to see others as nightmares or threats, we abdicate our responsibility to discover the gifts and passions which allow us to attain our destiny in Christ.

Rather than viewing people as gifts from God to the human community in which we live, envy makes the people around us potential threats. When I think of the times I have struggled with envy, I feel my jaw muscles getting tight and the muscles in my shoulders and neck tensing. My breathing becomes shallow. At other times, when envy strikes, I feel as if I might implode. But these physiological changes are a response to a perceived threat.

Why is it that we always seem to want what others have? Why am I six feet four inches tall, but often wish I were shorter to get into things that are down low, or perhaps be more comfortable on an airplane? It seems so silly when we see others paralyzed by envy, but we don't have to search too deep to find a good healthy dose of it in ourselves.

The sources of envy are not in the objects of envy, but rather in the misunderstanding of God and the realities of human life. Envy causes us to be wrongly introspective. Wrong introspection takes place when we compare ourselves to others. If we appreciate ourselves too much, we fall prey to pride. If we fail to appreciate our gifts, we fall prey to envy. Accurate introspection and reflection values the gifts of others and searches for ways to use the best of what one possesses. When we practice the wrong form of introspection it issues a statement to our maker: We thumb our nose at God and the gifts He has so graciously given us in this life.

You see, when we begin to envy others, we simultaneously begin to forget God. We forget that we are God's unique idea. We forget we have God-given talents that we are specially called to utilize in order to fulfill our destiny.

I have a deep passion for the sport of football and for music. I would love to be a pro football player or the lead guitar player in a really hot band. Having been a sports announcer, I have been exposed to more football envy than anything else.

One year while covering the Seattle Seahawks of the NFL, I went to training camp and witnessed an absolute phenomenon. His name was Curt Warner. He was a rookie running back from Penn State University. His talent for carrying the football was totally instinctual.

On the first day of training camp, Warner broke loose for big runs virtually every time he got the football. He seemed to run more like a UFO than a human. He stopped and started, dodged and darted, and changed directions at full speed. He went on to earn NFL Rookie of the Year honors.

Well, the press conference following that first day of practice was all about Curt. Seahawks coach, Chuck Knox, was asked what made the rookie so good. Knox's answer: "What you have seen there, gentlemen, is a God-given gift. Nobody can coach it. No one can learn it. It's a gift from God."

As a football wanna-be, I couldn't help but envy Warner's gifts and as I did so, I found myself saying, "I can't do anything the way he does football."

Here is where envy becomes a problem. I become so focused on someone else's assets that I disregard my own. Envy is a great tool to use to convince ourselves that we ought to just stop trying—to give up.

What we really want to have happen when we see greatness is to have it inspire greatness in us—to steel us to discover and use our gifts to make a stunning contribution to the world.

This is the lie built into the message that envy sends us. The fact is you are unique and gifted. There is something—or some things—that you do immensely better than others. Your gifts are needed. I am a pastor and communicator. Football and lead guitar are out, but I can make a contribution out of my gifts.

As with pride, envy embodies a misunderstanding of the character of God. First of all, when we find ourselves playing the comparison game and losing at it, we begin to denigrate our attributes. That's offensive to God, since our gifts, talents, and personalities come from the Creator. I fail to live in the reality that God loves me and guides my life in a way that everything works together for good. Envy spits at God's plan and aggressively states a new self-directed agenda for life.

There is a marvelous story in Matthew's Gospel. A wealthy businessman plans to go on a long journey. Before he leaves, he calls in three of his faithful employees. He gives them each a bundle of cash. You can imagine him saying, "I'm going on a trip. I like your style. So, here's ten thousand dollars to invest in my absence."

The boss makes the same gracious gift to two more of his trusted servants. All but one of them invest the money. One does a little better than the other, but when the boss returns, he tells them both, "Well done. Now I can trust you with even more."

But the last fellow comes up and says, "Here's your money. I buried it in the ground so that you could have all your principal back because I have heard that you are a mean and exacting man, and I didn't want to make you angry."

To this, the boss replied, "You're fired. Security, toss him out of here. The one who invests well will get more. Those who don't utilize opportunities like the one I have offered will not only fail to move ahead but they will lose the little that they already have."

I am more and more aware in my life that envy is a symptom of separation from God. The separation from perfect love shakes our foundations and makes us unstable. We don't know where to find love, or meaning, or purpose.

Here's the truth I find most illuminating on envy. At its core, envy comes from a misunderstanding of who God is. Imagine the three servants in Jesus' parable of the talents. Two servants think the master is a wonderful, gracious gift giver. They are free to risk, free from fear, empowered to succeed.

Then there's the third servant. Diametrically opposed to the first two servants, he gushes words of fear, judgment, distrust, and blame. Where in the world did this response come from? The essential message of the story is that the Master is a gracious giver and that we can leverage and capitalize on the gifts He has given us.

Envy makes us look away from what God has given us and question His wisdom. When I second-guess God about my personality, my body, my gifts, etc., I call into question God's good intentions for me. I also question God's ability to skillfully rule over Creation. Like the misguided investor in the story from Matthew, I easily begin to see God as cruel and exacting, nonunderstanding of my needs, wishes, and desires. In fear and disappointment, I bury my gifts and let them rot.

Envy is common, pervasive, and deceptive. You will remember from the discussion of pride that the sin of pride pollutes relationships by covering over and smothering the lives of others in the midst of a personal claim of superiority. Envy is a different process, but it leads to a similar degradation in human relationships.

When we envy someone for some reason, we wind up attaching ourselves to his or her story—sometimes even to the individual's life! We want what that person has got and we feel we deserve it. Watching others' success in deep green envy is painful. So we begin looking for opportunities to see the one we envy fall and be taken down a notch or two. Very few of us are able to contain a secret satisfaction inside ourselves at the misfortune of another.

Wishing the worst for those around us is the polluting social agent caused by envy. While the eyes of pride look down, the eyes of envy peek up through tiny little slits suspicious that someone nearby might just be getting something that the envious one isn't; paranoid that someone might be more capable in something than oneself.

You've heard, "You can be anything you want to be." I find that there is a pervasive idea in our society today that everybody ought to be able to be and do anything that they wish. We all want to have it all and do it all, and most of us want it *now*. Frankly, that doesn't work. But I wonder if our individualistic and materialistic society hasn't created a working myth, a fantasy, which cannot be corrected in our time.

A young woman in a church where I served some years ago had absolutely no musical talent. Yet she would say, "I have a bachelor's degree in musical performance and I should be teaching music somewhere."

I couldn't muster the heart to say, "I'm so sorry, but that's not you. You are very good with computers, video, and other creative endeavors."

One of the main reasons I remained silent regarding this person's talents was because she was so insecure, so arrogant, and so mean-spirited toward others that she was not ready to hear honesty regarding her gifts. In the meantime, her envy bloomed.

On numerous occasions, she said to me, "I could do that song better than Judy." Somehow, she had been sold the idea that if she thought it would be fun or fulfilling to do something, then she could just do it and attain competence.

Let's face it: We cannot do everything that we want to do. Yes, we can develop our strengths and accomplish plenty, but we have to work with the basic, raw materials God gave us at birth. We may make progress in personality, social skills, moral behavior, and vocational competence, but all the progress is dependent on our tapping into the "real us" rather than trying to emulate another person, or have a style forced upon us by the prevailing culture.

Those of you who grew up in the sixties will enjoy this story. One of my dear friends, John, was standing in front of his congregation when he took a section of Paul's letter to the Philippians and did an exposition of the text following the outline of an old song by the band Steppenwolf.

"Get your motor running," said John, "don't wait around. Get your life in God going." He went on, "Head out on the highway," which he embellished with "You can't grow at home. You have to head out. Getting your motor running in the garage and going nowhere is deadly."

He went on to inspire his large congregation with references from the song about adventure, adaptability, and a can-do attitude.

What a superb sermon! Stellar. I should have been overjoyed. But one symptom of envy that I experience is dejection. I see someone who is marvelously gifted and I just want to give up. My dear friend John is one of the best preachers in America. He's a genius. He writes his sermons in a short time yet they are delivered as finely tuned, deeply thoughtful communications. Many pastors massage sermons for twenty hours in a week and cannot contend with my friend's two or three hours of sermon preparation.

When I hear John preach, I am always amazed at the message, but often feel a bit dejected knowing that I am not as good a preacher as he is. I am stronger than John in a number of areas, but the dejection causes me to look only at the one issue. If this sounds a little like the sin of pride to you, you are correct. As I mentioned earlier, pride is an overly extravagant assessment of one's self. On the other hand, envy is an overly pessimistic assessment of one's self. If other people's success depresses you or me, we probably need to scan our hearts and minds for an infestation of envy. If another person's gifts make you want to abandon your gifts, then be ready to do battle with a bad case of envy.

An even nastier symptom of envy is that spiteful, malignant feeling, full of negative accusations, that comes our way. This level of envy poisons our souls and makes victims of all of our comrades as they witness our envy in action.

The movie *Amadeus* is the story of Mozart, arguably one of the great geniuses in the history of music. He was so good that, at a young age, he surpassed the greats of his day. In addition to professional brilliance, he was as wild as they come and as irresponsible as can be. One of the men he surpassed on his way to stardom was named Salieri.

At a party one night, Salieri was talking to other composers and musicians. He went on a tirade about Mozart's womanizing, boozing, and manic episodes. He then said something to the effect that this fiend, Mozart, sat down and played notes and put them on paper so fast that it simply looked sloppy. One of the party companions commented, "He must just be turning out junk to get the piece done in time."

Salieri responded, "No. It was like he was taking dictation from God. Every note perfect. Scarcely any corrections."

The inner hurricane of envy tears at the fabric of society. Rather than standing in awe of someone's ability to make music, earn money, invest assets, or lead organizations, envy causes us to become bitter. We pretend not to be watching those we envy, but we are watching and waiting for chances to make our move on them.

In Texas a teenage girl tries out for cheerleader. Her mother, an insecure and envious person, is determined to do anything, literally anything, to get her daughter on the cheerleading squad.

As the tryouts and voting approach, the mother becomes ever more the victim of envy. She can't stand the thought of anyone beating her daughter in the competition for slots on the cheerleading squad. Her fixation was focused entirely on her daughter's rival for this coveted position. In her jealousy, this obsessive woman arranged a contract killing to murder the mother of her daughter's teenage rival, thinking that the overwhelming grief over her mother's death would cause the rival to fail at cheerleading tryouts. This story is a close-up look at the dark, vindictive side of envy.

If this sounds spectacular, or like some characteristic of our modern, unrestrained society, think again. In the early pages of Genesis, there is a story of two brothers, Cain and Abel.

The biblical account says that Cain and Abel both gave offerings to God out of reverence to the Creator. God really liked Abel's offering, and God rejected Cain's. God simply made a choice at that time. There was no condemnation of Cain, nor was there a reason to believe that things would always be this way—Abel on top, Cain in second place.

Well, most of us know the story. Cain murders Abel so that his offerings will be the best that God can get from that point onward. I have often mused that this passage applies well to all of life, especially church life. Cain lived by the credo that "the way to get ahead is to eliminate the competition."

We don't know with certainty why Cain killed Abel as a reaction to God's rejection of his offering. But my best instincts tell me that jealousy and envy were at work.

Envy is wanting something that belongs to someone else. If this is true then jealousy is almost the same. Jealousy is not wanting someone to have what they've got. Because both envy and jealousy are preoccupations with others in a distorted behavior of comparison and analysis that results in serious problems.

Now, I don't know if you share my pathology or not, but one serious problem I have is self-condemnation. When we find ourselves practicing self-condemnation because we don't think we are as good as someone else, or because we covet that person's gifts, we can be sure we are moving into the province of the deadly sin of envy. I catch myself being envious and I proceed to roll up the proverbial newspaper and hit myself over the nose, snarling, "Bad dog! Bad dog!" But does whipping ourselves and practicing self-condemnation help? I don't think so. Self-condemnation comes out of a guilt- or shame-based approach to living. To the degree that I am suffering from envy at any given time, I also suffer from self-condemnation. Guilt and shame rule me.

Guilt is that alarm that goes off inside of us to say, "You have done a bad thing." But we become so sensitized to the voice of guilt that our response is, "See, I can't do anything right." The paralysis of guilt actually adds to our dejection and steers us away from healthy disciplines that can move us forward on life's journey.

Now, it would certainly be unwise to eliminate guilt altogether. Our very study of sin informs us that human nature is fractured, that we do wrong. And it might be useful to see guilt as a moral smoke alarm. When the fire of one of the Seven Deadly Sins is just a tiny thing, its smoke is enough to set off a well-tuned smoke alarm.

When the alarm goes off, we assess the source of the problem and act accordingly. Now, as all of us know, good smoke alarms must be fairly sensitive. That means we will have false alarms. So, when the guilt alarm rings inside of us we have to carefully examine whether our life is potentially going up in flames, or if the toast was just a little burnt. We are bound to get false alarms, but if we deal with them realistically, which in my case means making fun of my cooking and resetting the alarm, then everything is okay. But some of us don't want to use this response.

Tragically, the therapeutic model of personal development often denies the reality of a Creator, and from a secularized perspective places the locus of moral authority in the hands of the individual. We buy smoke alarms at Home Depot, so why not invest in moral and ethical smoke alarms? They are God-given. What I find so encouraging about responding to the alarms is that we can prevent further damage to us and others. We can avoid burning down the neighborhood with our sin. The therapeutic community's answer has all too often been, "Ignore the guilt. You don't have to feel guilty. Take responsibility for your life." In essence people are encouraged to remove the batteries from their internal smoke alarms and take a chance without this annoying device that goes off on all sorts of false fire reports. I say, listen to the guilt—respond to the real alarms, reset your conscience (smoke alarm) for false alarms, and be at the ready for the next sounding of the claxon. A true spiritual pilgrim wants to be well, longs to be well. And in the longing for wellness he or she welcomes all manner of nudgings which say, "It's time to deal with this."

Shame is even more diabolical than guilt. For, where guilt says to us, "You did a bad thing" (whether or not we have), shame says, "you are a bad person."

Both guilt and shame can have debilitating consequences if wrongly understood. Is guilt ever appropriate? Why, of course. It alerts me to a violation of my own value system and asks me to overcome the problem.

The technical name for this problem is cognitive dissonance. Cognitive dissonance is when two ideas and values are at war within us causing mental and emotional stress. The human psyche seeks resolution for cognitive dissonance. For instance, I say that I value treating all people with kindness and decency as much as possible. On the same day that I affirm this core moral value, I get run off to the shoulder of the road by a person who didn't see me as he merged into my lane.

I am making this story up for illustrative purposes, so let's be dramatic. I choose to get back on the road, cut off this person, and honk my horn. It feels so good to vent my anger, but a few minutes later, I start feeling pangs of guilt. "I didn't need to do that. Maybe he was blinded by the sun or couldn't see me the way his mirrors were adjusted. He probably felt terrible for almost causing a wreck, now here I am terrorizing him."

So, cognitive dissonance is what happens when our internal guilt and shame alarms go off. We get a message about what is putting a strain on our brain. Then, we must decipher the sources and be willing to say an assertive "no" to false guilt and shame, yet keep our alarm system tuned to act upon the proper forms of guilt.

Shame is trickier than guilt in the way that it plays, because we tend to universalize the "you are a bad person" message and bury ourselves emotionally, spiritually, and intellectually.

As a kid, I went on a crime spree. I was only about ten when I began stealing money from my parents. I was a careful investor for a thief: I put the money in my bank account. But when Dad went to make a gift deposit for me, he saw the deposits that had no understandable source of funding. He looked me in the eye and said, "Where did you get the money that you have been depositing?"

I answered, "From doing Grandma's yard."

Dad said, "You don't make that much there. Are you sure about your story?"

I said, "Yes," in a full-out lie.

Later that week, Dad left a pile of change sitting out on his dressing table. Little did I know that Dad had painted six quarters with fingernail polish, marking the money. I stole five of those marked quarters and deposited them into my savings account. When Dad came home, he realized that his money was missing and asked if I knew where his quarters were.

I said, "No," in another huge lie.

Dad asked again, and again, each time adding more evidence and giving me a chance to confess and move forward.

Again and again, I said, "No."

Then, my dad asked me to get my bankbook. I brought it to him and he asked where I got the money to make a deposit that day.

I said something like, "I dunno."

Well, I was caught red-handed. A thief. A liar. A rebel. A bad person. I was devastated by the magnitude of my own sin and the consequences of lost trust and confidence in me by my parents. I made things right by paying back the money, doing work around the house, asking forgiveness, and promising not to steal or lie again.

These acts of contrition became a learning experience for my future life. The positive acts of work to make amends were not a condition of my being forgiven, they were exercised out of the strength of already having been forgiven. The work I did is called restitution. My work restored the stolen money, restored my resolve to do right, and slowly began to restore my parents' trust in me.

But I still remember my sense of shame. It was overpowering. "I am a bad person." Again, I don't want to knock shame totally, because it has its role in human life. There are some things that are shameful. To hurt a child, to assault a spouse, to rape, to kill— these are cowardly, shameful deeds of which one ought to be good and ashamed. In fact, in the wake of office and school massacres, I often wonder if we wouldn't do better with a little more healthy sense of shame in our society.

But a better understanding of what a legitimate shame alarm ought to do within us will put us back on track to becoming the sort of person that we long to be. "I displayed the behavior of a bad person when I lied and stole, but now I value the truth and respect for private property. With God's help, I can learn, grow, and go forward from this."

To finish my personal shame story, I received a marvelous gift from my dad. When I was caught stealing I was to be grounded from all outings to the ice arena, or other social events. I had to come home after school. Worst of all, I was banned from my favorite activity: fishing. I was just whipping myself because I love to fish, and I was sure that with the horrible crime I had committed, my dad would never take me out for the opening day of trout season that was to begin in several weeks.

I can almost hear myself as a little boy saying to myself, "You will always be a loser and probably never get to fish or do anything with Dad again. It's over."

On Thursday night before the opening day of the lake fishing season, Dad came up to me after dinner and asked if I had my chores done and also confirmed that I had paid back all that I had stolen.

Dad announced, "Well, you better be packed and ready by dinnertime tomorrow night so we can head out to the lake and get ready for opening day."

I was blown away. What a gracious action. My dad saw that I was punishing myself and going into a funk, and he rescued me. He took me fishing and said on the trip that I was doing well and that we were now square on all accounts.

What a gift. My dad said, "You could have been taking steps to become a bad person, but you have learned your lesson."

My dad taught me about grace. Grace frees us from guilt and shame. Grace and love from God help us avoid partaking in the self-condemning messages that are derived from sin. God's absolute love for us puts up with sin, but even better, in His greatness, God pities us.

As a little boy I was thinking, "Other kids are good. I am bad. Other kids are honest. I am a liar. Other kids do things with their dads. I have ruined all that." But my father showed mercy and grace in restoring our time together and, thus, our relationship.

By the way, this is how God is with us and our shame. When we declare ourselves to be flawed, broken, losers, God says, "You are my idea. I created you. I love you absolutely. I love you perfectly. Nothing you could ever say or do could get me to love you more." God's cure for shame is to assure us that the shaming is no longer necessary.

One friend of mine summarized the Judeo-Christian tradition's message as "God loves you. Don't be stupid." This motto has some merit. We are invited to accept God's outrageous love, mercy, and forgiveness. And by intimate contact with God in prayer, worship, meditation, and study of Scripture, we gain the wisdom and new perspectives we need to become the sort of people God dreams for us to be. And the people that all of us, deep in our hearts, long to be.

I have written plenty about the pain and suffering caused by envy. Having come this far, we will turn our attention to various means of countermanding the effects of the second of the Seven Deadly Sins.

Perhaps one pathway through envy is self-discovery. Reflection can help us to understand who we are. Prayer, proper introspection, and engaging in the use of gifts shapes our understanding of our own uniqueness. There's certain joy in the discovery of one's gifts and passions. Living beyond shame and guilt and looking at the real you.

So, if we mustn't respond to envy and jealousy in our lives with shame and guilt, what resources do we have to combat this deadly sin?

If severe, personally imposed discipline doesn't do the job, then how about countermanding envy with something like contentment? Contentment is a virtue. But it's not the hygienic response to envy I always thought it was. Contentment is sort of an end-state. Contentment implies that we are free of envy. But how do we get there? By force of will? "Randy, just be content. Stop striving. Don't look at others." It never works. If God's Spirit is indeed at work in us, there must be some fruit of the Spirit that enhances our capability to be more content and less engaged in envy. Contentment is not something we can simply muster. It is the by-product of life enwrapped in joy. My personal discovery of the spiritual fruit of joy was life-transforming.

One night in the most unusual setting, I discovered and experienced the medicine that keeps envy in check. It is called joy. Joy is that sense of overall well-being and an inner knowledge that "all is well, everything is in its right place."

My wife, Nancy, and I were with some special friends at the ballet. The performance was Mozart's Divertimento 15.

It was beautiful. Nancy and our friends were almost cooing, "It's gorgeous! What grace!" We could barely sit still.

During the ballet, most of the cast was onstage all of the time, and the lead ballerina was exceptionally stunning. She was tall and rangy and moved smoothly, with uncommon strength and precision. In her quick and powerful movement, this dancer was absolutely riveting to watch. I turned to our friend, who was at one time a ballerina, and said, "She is absolutely out of this world."

Knowing ballet the way she did, my friend said, "She's perfect. Absolutely perfect in this role."

At the end of the performance I leaned over to my wife and our friends and said, "My God, that was beautiful! That is exactly what seeing someone release their gifts and talents to full potential is like. It was a thing of beauty that has somehow left a mark on me that will change me forever."

Nancy and I went home extolling the virtues of the ballerina. The next morning as I was working in my study, a thought struck me. Randy, why don't you view more of life as art? Why can't you see the artistry of everyday people about everyday things? When someone succeeds in a job situation, why don't you celebrate it with an effervescent joy the way you did at the ballet?

My answer was that I lacked joy. I didn't look for the beauty, the harmony, and the overwhelming points of grace in life because I was not the awestruck ballet-goer. Instead, I was the critic. I was looking at others, judging performances, comparing myself to others, feeling superior in one situation and inferior in another.

I realized that I had tuned myself—body, mind, and soul—to look for the negative, rather than searching for glimpses of grace. It's been a hard transition for me in the years since that night at the ballet, but I am trying to see everyone's life as something aesthetic, a source of beauty, a unique art form.

Seeking joy in our lives is rewarded by Joy from our Master. Joy is the overall love of life and everyone who's alive. Aristotle didn't use the word joy in his seven virtues, but he does use the words great spiritedness. Great spiritedness corresponds directly with Paul's idea of joy. Great spiritedness says we are open-minded, appreciative of others, accepting of our own potential for both goodness and havoc.

I mentioned in the last chapter that holding sin in check is a bit like flossing one's teeth daily. It takes a steady discipline. The sources of decay will never go away, but flossing holds them at bay.

Here are some tips for how to institute joy in your passage through this world, thus reducing the presence of envy. First of all, go back to the concept of God. Refocus your life on God rather than on yourself. Realize that God has created a world of beauty. Look for the beauty. Look for the art that is all around you.

Second, tune into the fact that God is crazy about you. By prayer and statements of faith like, "I am alive because you made me, God, and I am living to bring joy to your heart." Give in to the idea that you are unique and special.

Third, we all must endeavor to discover and unleash our unique gifts whether they are music, drama, business, law, medicine, parenting, carpentry, ministry, or writing. We all have gifts. When we intentionally discover and deploy our gifts, we make serious progress in the business of self-acceptance, and our eyes tend to start moving away from the envy of others.

He was known as the Flying Scotsman. Eric Liddell was a

Christian missionary and Olympic-class runner who later competed in the 1924 Olympics. You probably remember his story from the movie *Chariots of Fire.*

As the story goes, Liddell was home from China with his sister, raising funds for their mission and ministering to the Scottish folk that they had befriended.

Liddell was winning some important foot races, and he was considering the Olympics. His sister urged him to drop running and turn his energies to the missionary enterprise that he came home to do, because God had gifted him to excel in the ministry.

His sister said, "We need you here. God's made you for this."

Eric Liddell's recorded response is a classic. To the comment that God made him for ministry, he replied, "Aye . . . and He also made me fast! And when I run, I can feel His pleasure."

Feeling God's pleasure as our gifts and talents are put to use surely evicts guilt and shame from our lives and introduces a quality of joy so deep and abiding that envy simply gets edged out. There is little room for envying others when we are caught up in joy. God's pleasure in us is a far better motivator than the comparison game we play in envy. It's always positive and consistently the cause of forward momentum.

We have the opportunity to look at other people's lives as a work of art. Try to take someone you envy and celebrate their gifts and their uniqueness. This is not touchy-feely sentimental stuff—it really works. Reframing our thinking with one object of envy can transform that green, venomous inner monster into admiration and appreciation grounded in joy over the wonders of life.

As we do this reframing process one case at a time, we build up our receptivity to joy and appreciation. It's amazing; we actually become the persons we long to be. We gradually become more and more sensitive to the presence of beauty and joy around us, and our once-wandering and envious eyes are opened to a whole new world.

The sins we love take root in our lives through long-term thought patterns and behaviors that we justify. We actually believe that sins like envy make us more of a person. So, we love the sin and make a joke of it. In the end, the joke is on us.

Envy is a deadly sin. It seriously cripples us spiritually, emotionally, and socially. Joy, imparted to us by the Holy Spirit, gives a new set of eyes with which to view life. And the sins we used to love, like envy, fade in the light of love emerging in you and in me.

FIVE

You'd Be Mad Too: ANGER

Back in the mid-1980s, I was a partner in a company that produced videos and live events. We often taxed our bodies and minds to the maximum. On one trip we were shooting footage in Seattle, Washington, D.C., Chicago, Richmond, Virginia, Atlanta, Houston, Denver, and Los Angeles with less than a one-day stop at each location.

I remember looking at my partner and saying, "I feel like I'm losing control of myself. I'm so exhausted." He admitted that he felt about the same and then our conversation was interrupted as we turned into the Los Angeles International Airport and had to unload tons of video gear which we had hauled through some of the largest airports in the United States during the past week.

As we checked our bags and gear at the ticket counter, an agent informed us, "Your camera cases are over the allowable seventy-five pounds. You have to pay three hundred dollars extra per case." We had about twenty minutes until our plane was scheduled to leave. And the absurdity was that we always packed the cases the same way, and we had not ruled overweight in any other city. I asked for a supervisor, but the ticket agent refused.

Almost all of us can relate to this sort of high-stress, boil-over situation. It's probably no surprise to anyone that I totally lost it with the ticket agent. It got loud and nasty. Supervisors were called in. In the end, we got to load our stuff as it was for no extra charge. But what did I win?

As you may have experienced in these situations, I won the battle but lost the war. My business partner was angry with me, saying, "You were a real jerk." A dear and trusted friend had his confidence in me rattled and was embarrassed by my behavior.

I felt horribly guilty. My adrenal glands were pumping about a gallon per second, and my body felt as if it was running on jet fuel. And, in the long run, there was no mistaking that I was the one with a problem.

I raged. My wrath hurt God, others, and myself. Anger is like that. It's hot and toxic. Its scars remain on all those who are inadvertently standing too close to us when anger erupts.

The third deadly sin, anger, is also called rage and wrath, I might add to that the word frustration, because frustration is a form of anger to which we have given dignity and appropriateness as a sort of pre-anger.

Obviously there are different levels of anger, but lest we fall prey to the temptation to grade anger by intimating that our frustrations (which we nurture and stew upon and lead to much anger) are not as bad as two motorists screaming at each other on the highway. Well, sorry to tell you, that isn't how this problem of sin works. You and I can't just sin with anger a little and call it okay, then draw some imaginary line of when anger is really a problem.

My suspicion is that earlier writers referred to anger as rage and wrath because they wanted to increase the seriousness of how we identify and deal with all angry feelings. The fact is that our anger, whether we call it frustration, being miffed, hurt, enraged, or full of wrath has devastating consequences upon you, me, and our world.

One of the backsides of anger that is so damaging is that once we have dumped our anger on someone else, it usually comes back after us. I begin to feel guilty and ashamed when I have blown up. I hate who I am when I express anger inappropriately. I cannot even conceive of how to discuss it with those I have hurt or revisit the circumstances for self-improvement. The flame of anger flashes outward, but the same flame licks away at the heart, soul, and mind of the person who expresses rage.

Pride and envy may be secret sins that we can mask and disguise, but run-away anger is a public event. There is no way to truly hide it. Sometimes people attempt to seethe quietly. They kid themselves into believing that no one can tell they are angry. Or, they express their anger as concerns and intellectualize it. Intellectualization of anger attempts give anger a justifiable, sweet smell, but the noxious, toxic poison of anger cannot be hidden, only shoddily masked. Frankly, our attempts to hide anger just don't work well at all. It's always there, just below the surface. In fact, some of us are experts at turning our toxic barrage inward. Psychologists say that much of depression is anger turned inward. Such inward anger pollutes our soul and later finds its way into our social networks. There is no getting around the reality of anger. There is no way to prevent rage from taking its toll without careful attention to our anger. If we are going to bring the perfect love of God to the angry places in our lives, we need to know what we are angry about. We also need to understand the triggers which initiate anger in us.

Anger occurs when a human being perceives a threat. The threat can be real or perceived. It emanates from the brain stem and is very much a primal emotion. It is intricately connected to the human body's "fight or flight" instincts. When a person perceives a threat, adrenaline starts pumping, painkilling and strength-enhancing hormones surge, blood pressure increases, blood flow moves to the vital organs, and the body prepares for the effort of a lifetime.

The decision involved in this primal, survival response is "Do I stay and fight, or run for my life?" In the face of a threat, the body prepares itself for either. Earlier in the history of the human race this handy response allowed a person to flee a charging animal or empowered a person to fight a Herculean battle with the likes of a saber-toothed tiger. These days, all those same fight or flight responses happen any time we are threatened.

Anger is a response to threat. When a coworker says something disrespectful to us or a ticket agent at an airport becomes belligerent over the weight of bags, we feel threatened. We feel that our space or our rights are threatened when we get cut off in traffic or a supermarket line. And we respond in fight or flight.

Think for just a minute about all of the body responses that happen when fight or flight is triggered. They all indicate short-term, high-stress loads on the body. How often do we want to trigger these powerful agents? My wife has had two children and has experienced the fluctuations in hormones. From her description, it's no picnic for her or the people around her. It wears on a person. Similarly, when we fire up fight or flight, it takes its toll upon us. It wears out our systems and pushes the cardiovascular, muscular, and nervous systems to the maximum.

So, a fundamental question for all of us is—how many things are there that threaten us, and what are they? I can be threatened by change, rejection, abandonment, exclusion, alienation. How about you? What gets your goat? Why? MAy differ w/ people ,

A quick disclaimer before we go further. I am in no way saying that all anger is bad. In fact, just as pride and envy trigger guilt smoke alarms in our lives, anger fires off a warning that all is not as it should or could be. That trigger is often missed. Anger becomes problematic at just this point. When the anger clarifies an issue of importance to us and moves us to reconciliation with the source of our anger, it is positive. When anger becomes all-consuming, it is called rage. Rage doesn't seek to reconcile, rather it seeks to destroy the person or object causing the anger. We practice this type of rage all too often in our culture. We marvel at road rage when angry drivers open fire on other motorists with handguns. But many of us kill and maim others on a daily basis with our nonreconciling use of anger.

On the issue of reconciling anger, Paul speaks God's words in Ephesians: "Be angry but do not sin. Don't let the sun go down on your anger." What Paul tells us is that we have to recognize anger when we are experiencing it. At a second level we are to process our anger at an inner level and with other parties involved. Third, we are to process anger by the event and by the day, not allowing large reservoirs of anger to build within us. This is called keeping short accounts. Finally, we let the sun go down on the day and sleep off the strains of one day and move to the next with some peace of mind. This is how reconciling anger works. It actually puts us in touch with problems we face internally and problems that manifest themselves in our relationships with others. By committing to work on the problems, we actually create the opportunity for a deeper understanding of self and more intimacy with others. In this way, anger can be reconciling.

A man who does some work in the church I pastor was practicing some behaviors that really were making me angry. I knew I needed to speak up, but do so in a reconciling way. When I did confront him, it all exploded. "Why don't you take a look at yourself. You talk about problems. You love to hear yourself talk in your sermons!"

I politely reminded him that the topic on the table was not my sermons, but rather his behavior. In spite of my efforts to keep the first meeting nontoxic, things really blew up.

My fellow church leader said, "I'm out of here!" He stormed out the door and would not speak to me for at least two weeks.

I prayed and thought a lot about what was going on with me, with him, with us. I called him and asked if we could get together over dinner with one of our elders as a referee. Thank God he agreed.

Dinner was being served as I said, "You know I love you, and value your gifts. But this particular behavior you exhibit is out of bounds. I'm all for you. I am saying no to one behavior."

After much discussion, we got back on the same page and moved forward in the life of the church together. Our anger was behind us. Our future was ahead of us. And the anger actually served as a great clarifying tool.

Now, while the Ephesians model offers us the one workable way of processing anger, there are numerous nonreconciling forms of anger.

(1) One of those nonreconciling ways is to use anger to create boundaries. We use anger to get revenge. We use anger to justify our claim as victims. We use anger in many nonproductive ways. And we rationalize anger like crazy.

I cannot tell you how many times I have sat in my office with a hurting person and heard him or her say, "You would be mad, too, wouldn't you?" I never know how to answer that question, because the issue is not so much being mad as it is how one handles the anger."

A woman whose husband deserted her over twenty-five years ago drives a car with stickers all over it bearing epithets against ex-husbands. A quarter of a century is an awfully long time to rage against someone and store up bitterness. Think of the cumulative stress effect and the terrible erosion of a person's energy in such a circumstance.

Anger is not bad in itself, but it can turn bad without careful attention to expression and timing. Anger is best expressed as a
(1) "when you did [behavior], I felt [your feeling] and that made me

[outcome]." This puts us in a position of owning our anger. And it does one other thing ever so subtly: It makes us focus rationally on emotion. How's that for a weird twist? But think about it, so many times when we are enraged, we either vent pure, irrational emotion, or we side step emotion altogether and try to make it look as if our anger is purely objective. We feel that letting someone who has stepped on our toes see our hurt or insecurity will only give them more ammunition to load and use on us. But the fact is that we don't make progress until we own the subjective side of anger. "This is the emotion I am experiencing as a result of _____." So, the "when you . . ." formula gets us to own and articulate our emotions up front.

There are a couple of other things about anger worthy of mentioning. Not all relationships where anger is present are safe, nor are they reconcilable. The fact is that there are dangerous, harmful people in this world. When encountering such people, we do best to ask God to forgive them and plead with God to bridle their behavior and then walk away, leaving God in charge.

The simple "When you . . ." formula is outstanding because it helps us talk about our anger in a way that makes us take responsibility for our anger response. I no longer say, "I had a right to get mad because you're an idiot." Instead, I find myself saying, "Given the way I am wired, this really ticked me off."

I pastor a somewhat innovative church in a very traditional denomination. I overheard a conversation between two ministers whom I didn't know well. Frankly, I didn't have the deepest respect for them to begin with. And then I heard them talking about me and the church that I pastor in quite negative and condescending tones. My threat alarms went off at full force. I didn't know whether to stomp out of the room, sneak out of the room, or launch a verbal fusillade against my two colleagues.

I decided to confront them assertively with the "When you . . ." formula. I said, "Excuse me for interrupting, but I believe I just heard you talking about me and my church. When you do that without ever having visited the church or questioning me, I feel very disrespected and it lowers my desire to be invested in relationships at the denominational level." The result was a frank conversation and some progress in our relationships.

I wish I could say this is what I always desire, but it's not. There is a sick part of me that wanted to verbally shred these two colleagues, to insult and humiliate them, to teach them not to mess with me. I still can't believe that I experimented with the right thing for once.

So, anger must be expressed properly to be productive. At a second level, timing is an issue. Anger is best managed in a timely fashion. Unresolved and unprocessed anger does not go away. It ferments. It boils. It's not even good to heed conventional wisdom and "sleep on it."

The way to keep anger from becoming vindictive, embittering, and rage-expressing is to deal with it in a timely manner.

We need short accounts. The alarms we sense from pride, envy, and anger all demand us to act *now*. They are not like the light on our dashboard which tells us that we have sixty more miles' worth of gas in our tank. Anger is a true alarm.

Let me also say that anger doesn't have to be a spewing, violent, verbal rage to be deadly. Passive-aggressive anger is a quiet, seething anger that looks for payback through circuitous routes. Its consequences are no better than those caused by a more outward and volatile expression of anger.

Anger destroys first the one who is perpetually angry. Anger is

a death sentence to peace of mind, good health, and the ability to
appreciate life. Yet, we live with it day in and day out rationalizing,
by saying "You'd be angry too if this happened to you."

I have several mentors in my life. One of those is Dr. Bruce Larson, a well-known author, speaker, pastor, and spiritual pilgrim.
Bruce and I were once talking about an angry dispute a mutual
friend was involved in.

Bruce said, "You know, Randy, we all take some hard hits in
life. We get mad at different offenses, but when it comes to anger,
the secret to life is asking the question, 'Do you want to be right or
do you want to be well?'" Do you want to be right or do you want to
be well? It's a good question for those of us Christians who tend to
think that we are right because we are aligned with God and we
must defend God and God's causes. We believe in truth and forget
that Jesus is the truth, not ourselves. We ramp up rage in our vehe-
ment commitment to be right. We fail to realize that the grace and
mercy of God is rooted in the fact that though God has the sovereign and justifiable right to exterminate His Creation for its sinful,
fallen status, he chooses to be well rather than be right, by an extreme definition of right. In other words, God, who wishes us well,
becomes one of us in Jesus Christ, lives among us, dies for us, and
offers the glorious, forgiving power of His death and resurrection to
us. Isn't that exciting, a righteous God opts for wellness.

Right or well? This is an important question. If we possess an
obsessive need to always be right, we will never let go of any offense, nor will we moderate the number and types of threats that
send our alarms chirping.

Being right versus being well is quite a tension, but it is fundamental. When we shape our thinking by placing too much value on
our interpretation of right and wrong, and our right to judge others
for their actions, we are locked into a self-centered thought system.

It is a system that denies the design of life and violates the principals of God, in whose image we are made.

If I want to be right, I can make a career of doing so through the ascent of my will and the strength of my personality. To be well, I must handle things God's way.

When it comes to anger, it appears to me that God's way to wholeness rests in developing a deep knowledge of the character of God and also knowing ourselves so well that we go beyond the rationalization games we can so easily play. Self-knowledge makes us aware of the crutches we use, the lies we tell ourselves, and also the triggers that cause us to act dysfunctionally (read act sinfully). Anger is part of a natural response pattern in our lives to threats. Yet, in our brokenness, we tend to affirm uses of anger that destroy. And we justify ourselves by saying, "You'd be mad too." When we realize what a grand excuse we have manufactured for our anger, it becomes all that much easier to actually increase the number and intensity of our rage behaviors. Suddenly, anger, one of the Seven Deadly Sins becomes one of the sins we love.

One of the first Protestant theologians, John Calvin, felt that all of life comes down to making progress by acquiring God-knowledge and self-knowledge. He said, "Our wisdom, in so far as it ought to be deemed true and solid wisdom, consists almost entirely of two parts: the knowledge of God and ourselves . . . but as these are connected together by many ties, it is not easy to determine which of the two precedes and gives birth to the other. No person can survey themselves without . . . turning their thoughts toward the God in whom they live and move . . . and . . . the infinite good which resides in God becomes more apparent from our poverty."

Our sinful broken condition leads us into the hands of a gracious and loving God. Our knowledge of God's love and grace frees us to do self-exploration.

These two sources of wisdom, God and self, are strange bedfellows indeed, but I believe Calvin is correct. As I explore myself, I become acutely aware that much of the anger I experience is self-generated and unwarranted. It's a false alarm as far as alarms go. I don't need to confront or change someone else. I need to change me. Also, I have learned to call anger what I have previously rationalized to myself as "frustration" and "irritation." These were my vain attempts to minimize my anger, give it a new name, and somehow slip under God's radar.

As I move from self-knowledge to God-knowledge, how can I not be fascinated by the magnitude and sovereignty of God? God is magnificent. All-loving. All-powerful. All-knowing. Ever-present. Perfectly wise. The list of God's attributes goes on and on. So, every time I begin reading the Scriptures, I know that I am learning about an awesome God. But probably no trait of God is more remarkable and awesome than God's patience. In the Old Testament it is called "long-suffering"—which creates a nice word picture.

God is patient with us in the midst of our tomfoolery. Whether we sin with malicious intent or foolishly slip up, God is patient. I often shock people when I talk around the country by saying, "God isn't mad anymore. Any anger God may have had toward the human race was deposited in the God-Man, Jesus, on a cross two thousand years ago."

People's jaws literally drop. Wow! God isn't mad? So many of us think God is standing around the corner from us, hidden and waiting to annihilate us for our most recent wrong. Yet, this misunderstanding of God is probably more offensive to God than the other sins we might commit. God isn't waiting to judge us. God is cheering for us and waiting to forgive us and reconcile with us. Paul's second letter to the Corinthian church says, "God chose not to hold our sins against us, but instead chose to become sin on our behalf in Jesus Christ so that you and I might be reconciled to God."

This is where the character of God becomes a model for you and me as we try to manage anger. First of all, a God like the one I am describing is a God with whom we can express the depth of our anger, hurt, and perceived threats.

If you read the New Testament Gospels that describe the life and teachings of Jesus Christ, you will see a Jesus who's not above anger. He angrily reprimands friends, he issues scathing fusillades against his detractors. The Old Testament paints a portrait of a perfectly loving God who is not above expressing anger.

The difference between divine anger and our anger and rage is the reason for the anger and the process for handling the anger. When Jesus used whips to expel money changers from the Temple in Jerusalem, his anger was the backside of love. He was offended on behalf of spiritual pilgrims who were being ripped off at the house of God, paying exorbitant taxes and fees in order to gain access to the worship of God. Affronts to God of this gravity don't go unaddressed by Jesus. But we also notice in Jesus that in addition to a right reason for anger, he handles it the right way. He is direct. He is honest. He takes responsibility for his anger.

(2) Second, when we confess our excess anger to God (instead of striving to somehow rationalize our right to be angry), he is able to hear our confessed sin and offer us forgiveness, which provides a clean slate and solid working capital in a relationship. And In turn, our experience of God's grace and forgiveness moves us to want to practice grace and forgiveness toward those around us. Working out what God has worked deep inside of us is a powerful anger suppression system.

Believe me it works. I run hot. I can be easily angered, but this enterprise of self-exploration and meditation on the character of God is really helping. Do not:

*Admission of sin is critical in human spiritual progress. To deny or rationalize sin is to severely damage an entire system of relationships. If I go to a counselor and lie to her, what good have I done? Can she help me? No. Do I get better? No. Well, then why would we try to cover up or rationalize sin with God? (Oh yeah, the God who knows it all anyway.) God simply asks us to confess our sins of anger and look deep inside for insights. God empowers us with grace to act upon anger more quickly and with an appropriate and helpful expression of the anger to the party causing us injury.

We can learn to utilize anger as a tool for growth. If it has that potential, why would I allow anger to be a tool for self-destruction, the pollution of relationships, the pathology it can create in personalities? The answer is that most of us like being right a hell of a lot more than we like being well.

Along the way, I have discovered a wonderful tool for lessening the frequency of anger. It takes some work. It is called the A+B=C formula. Here's how it goes: A equals an activating event. B equals a deeply held personal belief. C equals a consequence. This may sound like one of the physics theorems you worked with in high school. But let's look at it in light of the business of anger management. Let me try an example from real life.

"I am outraged. You guys were putting me and my husband down because we don't have the financial resources you have," Donna shouted at me.

I was visiting with this fine woman, who seethed with anger about events at a recent dinner party that we had attended. She was outrageously angry at one guest and mad at me.

Here's what had happened. During the dinner, the subject of our children's educations came up in our conversation. One parent, Barb, whose kids are quite shy and passive said, "I just had to put my kids in private school. It costs a lot, but if you love your kids that's what you will do."

I affirmed Barb's decision saying, "That's great." My own kids were in public school just like Donna's, but I understood Barb's sentiment.

But now, two days later, Donna was extremely angry both with me and Barb. Why? People were simply telling stories about their lives.

Looking at the belief system dynamics, check out Donna's response and my response. The activating event is the same for both the woman and myself. (A) A fellow guest at a dinner party (Barb) says loving her kids is sacrificing to sending them to private school. The belief system (B) of Barb and myself was very different, though I recognized that her kids might not do well in public school and admired her choice for her kids and her sacrifice. But to Donna, Barb was being a social-elitist with her talk of private schools and sacrifice. Donna felt that Barb was subtly putting everyone else down for not sending their kids to private school, and also intimating that those who send kids to public schools are selfish and unwilling to make sacrifices, or worse, don't *really* love their kids.

Now we get down to consequences (C) on the right side of the equals sign. My consequent reaction to the mixture of the activating event and my beliefs was that the private school mom's words made me want to renew my intentions to keep tabs on my kids' education and do whatever I could to help them. To Donna, it seemed to trigger a feeling of condemnation and deprivation, making her want to scream and shout and curse at Barb, then stomp out of the dinner and leave her current circle of friends.

Ultimately, Donna could not modify her belief systems to come in line with reality as God has made it and did in fact leave her friendship group. Her belief system caused her to assume that she was being put down. Her oversensitivity and insecurity prevented her from entering into any sort of civil conversation. She later left her church, descended into a massive depression, and last time we spoke she was frighteningly alienated. What a sad story.

Rage is the third of the Seven Deadly Sins, and like pride and envy before it, there is a virtue we can develop to keep our anger in check. It is called gentleness. It is one of Aristotle's classic virtues and it is listed in the New Testament as a fruitful representation of love in action.

Interestingly, gentleness has to do with putting ourselves in the other person's shoes and treating that person no more forcefully than absolutely necessary. In fact, gentleness understates claims and may lead us to strategies that fail to get our point across. But that's okay. Damage is minimized. This goes back to the earlier issue of whether we want to be right or well. Gentleness cultivates wellness in ourselves and in our social relationships. Gentleness is not overly assertive, but instead appropriately assertive, or perhaps even a little under-assertive. Gentleness focuses our efforts to deal with angry feelings by helping us seek reconciliation rather than revenge.

We develop gentleness as we rely on God's help and prayerfully work the A+B=C formula. You have probably gathered by now that we can't do much to change activating events in our lives. We try and try to find greener pastures and better relationships and to put up tremendous defenses, but the activating events are everywhere. Consequences are a direct result of activating events paired with belief systems. My kids are in public school and friends discuss the merits of private school for their kids and I'm thinking, cool. God bless these folks.

Gentleness is expressed when we modify our belief system. My wife has taught me a lot about working the A+B=C formula. She has a deep and abiding love for God and a sincere appreciation for other people. While I am driving behind an eighty-year-old lady getting all bent out of shape with her slow driving, Nancy says kindly, "That poor dear, I think the late afternoon sun is in her face blinding her." Nancy makes a judgment that expresses compassion for the little old lady. I practiced judgment, too, by condemning the woman. Nancy's judgment is kinder, gentler, reconciling.

Scripture tells us that "perfect love casts out all fear." No greater truth can be expressed when it comes to dealing with our anger. God's perfect love helps us tame our fears and deal with anger. You see, much anger is the result of fear.

My city of Seattle received a terrible black eye as a result of rioting during a World Trade Organization meeting. Poor planning, lack of security forces, and bad communication and decision making resulted in a real mess. Protesters with justifiable causes lined the streets and staged events. A small group of anarchists attacked buildings, set Dumpsters afire, and harassed the police.

Law enforcement agents from the police, National Guard, and State Patrol were left to basically freelance with a huge mob. One police officer who attends our church went about thirty-six hours without sleep. The cops were tired, outnumbered, and frustrated. They were also afraid. Can you imagine facing an angry mob and wondering what they might do?

Sadly, some of the police officers lost their cool and acted out in anger toward protesters and even news reporters. People were struck, shoved around, hit with pepper spray.

My diagnosis of this entire event: fear. Fear arouses our fight or flight instincts. It screams, *"Threat! Threat! Threat!"* When we respond to the alarm fear rings, we may retreat, but are more likely to respond in an overly assertive, take-charge manner that embodies the deadly sin of anger.

But, you see, perfect love casts out all fear. Again, we see that love is the hygienic treatment for all sin. Love manifested as gentleness is the preferred fruit of the Spirit for dealing with our anger.

(1)

When we believe that God is for us, therefore no one can truly be against us, we lighten up. When we study sin as we are doing between the covers of this book, our belief system changes. Suddenly I see my flaws much more clearly and am willing to accept the mistakes and flaws of others. (2) I begin to believe that others have a right to navigate their way through this world without my permission and certainly without my condescension.

(3) We also do begin to pity others. This is not condescending. It is empathetic. Empathy is identifying with the plight of another.

I walked out of the Kingdome in Seattle following a Seattle Seahawks football game. As I headed to the parking lot, I witnessed a man taking swings at a woman. Both had children standing by and the woman's husband was paralyzed by fear.

I don't know what started the fight, but I have a serious problem with men hitting or even threatening to hit women.

An inner voice, I believe the Holy Spirit, spoke to me and said, "Go and stop this fight in a way that honors both parties."

A large crowd stood by. They weren't thinking reconciliation, I am convinced they wanted to see the fight. Why break it up?

I stepped between the man and the woman and looking at the man said, "You're better than this. You don't want to be arrested for assault. Your son's with you, you have had a great day together. Just take him home and forget this, no matter what it's about. You will like yourself a lot better tomorrow if you do."

As the situation continued, I put my body between the two warring parties and actually took a punch, but kept repeating, "You don't want to do this. This cannot possibly be the real you."

Eventually, the two parties went their ways. And, I had the wonderful feeling that comes from being a reconciler.

As I reflected on this angry situation, I became more and more aware of the times my anger has been toxic. The story about me and the ticket agent screaming at each other over baggage weight that I told earlier in this chapter is just one example. I found my heart strangely tender toward the two people fighting in the Kingdome parking lot.

Because I frequently do the inexcusable and need to be forgiven, I begin to believe it is right to forgive others. Patience grows. I begin reacting angrily to an ever-lessening number of activating events. And rather than trying to manipulate events and consequences, I find myself digging deep into my own belief system and systematically telling myself the truth about things where once I told lies.

I grew up in an extended family with no college graduates. A great, great grandfather in Wales who was a physician was the most recent college graduate in our family. I figure he worked and retired before the American Civil War.

I value education. I wasn't always terribly diligent in studies, but I knew I wanted to study liberal arts, particularly the humanities. My goal was to know more and use the power of knowledge to achieve success.

Well, I am sorry to say that I developed a bad belief system. I began looking down my nose at the less educated. One day a friend in my small support group blasted me: "You disregard everyone that's not of the intelligentsia." I was shocked to hear those words, but as I sat there, speechless, I realized he was absolutely right. I embarked on a three- or four-year process of changing my beliefs by engaging a greater variety of people. We can use these same principles of reframing our belief system to work on our anger issues.

When you and I experience anger, we can try to access gentleness. The way to do this is by asking, "What do I believe or expect that is causing me to become angry?" If it's a legitimate reason, get mad. Gently express your anger to the offending party and ask for a different behavior. But we must act on our anger with gentleness.

God has been gentle and patient with us in the midst of our sinfulness. God has been gracious, and God is shaping us to be able to
extend these same qualities into our relationships, especially at
such crucial and difficult times as when we are angry.

Gentleness leads you and me to avoid venting anger, because
we know that words can really hurt and, once spoken, can't be
taken back. It doesn't work to try to reverse what has already been
said. Gentleness develops a quality of calmness in us that buys a
little time to process our angry feelings instead of just venting them
in a primal scream.

A couple of gentleness exercises I have been working on include my actual approach to people. First, I am going back to what
my mom taught me. "Bite your tongue, hold your breath, count to
ten, then consider saying something." This discipline of letting the
brain stem function of anger subside a little before we respond to a
dig made against us or to an anonymous insult which sparks issues
like road rage.

We can actually learn to stop. Reflect, ever so briefly. Then, we
can act rather than react with a much higher level of control.

When I have been offended and am considering expressing
anger, I ask myself several questions: What is the source of my
anger? What threat am I perceiving? How much of this is mine and
how much of this is theirs? Further, it's good to ask, Is this an issue
that must be confronted or could I forgive this person, let it go, then
speak up if it happens again? Most of us feel that when someone
has done something that makes us angry, they are supposed to be
aware of their offense, sorry for it, and perfectly willing to come to
us and ask forgiveness. If you have been trying this approach, you
may already be very frustrated by the lack of results. Now remember, we may choose not to process anger with the person who has offended us. If someone honks his horn at me on the freeway and
makes an obscene gesture, I don't have to do anything about it ex-

cept keep driving. It's not that big a deal. But if a friend says something very unkind to me, it may hurt and make me angry, causing damage to the relationship. It is incumbent upon me to express my anger to my friend. I need to vocalize what violation I perceived, tell about how it makes me feel, and about the consequences such a behavior has on our relationship. God calls us to manage our own anger, not make it the responsibility of someone else.

(4) If it is something I feel I must address with someone, how softly can I state the issue and still get my point across? This act of gentleness prevents us from dropping a fifty-megaton bomb when the pop of a cap gun would be more than enough to generate careful attention.

(5) Hearing anger is never fun. So, I have begun asking myself, "If I had to hear what I am going to tell this person, how would I best receive it from them?" This is empathy. Empathy and gentleness work together. Gentleness pushes no harder than necessary. Gentleness focuses on the style and results of interaction. Empathy is being in the other person's shoes, a place where we discover the sensitivities of others and learn to communicate with them in ways they can comprehend, accept, and respond to.

(6) Another important thing that I have learned about anger is that we should never express it against the character of a person. That is shaming. Shaming is bad. It sends someone a message that he or she is a bad person. If your adversary suffers from shame, she will either rebel against your shame statement and come at you full force, or she will take it as a shame message, internalize it, and descend into a black hole of self-hatred from which she may not soon emerge. When confronting someone, it is always best to focus on one specific behavior. Avoid the urge to say, "You always" or "You never."

(7) Gentleness sounds weak. The very vocalization of the word makes us speak in glowing, warm, and hushed tones. Forget that

reading of gentleness. It's faulty. Gentleness is actually way more powerful a force than aggression. This is so because aggression runs out of control in service of the self, while gentleness musters resources or self-control in service of the greater good.

(8)   Gentleness is proactive and intentional. Rage and aggression overcome us, wrestle us to the floor, sublimate our dignity, and then spew their acid rain on others.

(9)   Gentleness is a choice. It is an act of faith that we can make relationships work and an act of faith that acknowledges the presence of God in our world. Gentleness says, I am going to try to do things God's way. I think I will behave toward others the way God behaves toward me, even when I am being a goof up.

(10)   Gentleness is also intentional. Gentlepersons don't let anger slide. They love good relationships and the feeling of wholeness way too much. So, gentleness expresses itself as the one to schedule and open a reconciling dialogue.

As I think about the "When you . . ." formula and the "A+B=C" formula, I realize that the key to managing anger is developing a deep knowledge of ourselves and exercising just enough self-control to allow these formulas to be put to use. I chuckle as I see the face of my Norwegian grandmother saying, "Count to ten, Randy." Not bad advice.

Counting to ten means staying in control. Counting to ten means taking responsibility for the anger that has been triggered in you. Anger is caused by adrenaline flowing in massive doses in our body. Everything is pumping at a hundred plus percent. Forcing ourselves to stop and think before expressing our anger is an act of restraint that pays big dividends. We save ourselves from blowing up when we are not justified. We measure our words in ways that mend, rather than in ways that rip.

I would like to believe that you and I can live life beyond brain stem, primal functions. There has to be some use for all of that mass of gray tissue above the stem.

The evolution of the human person is a move from brain stem, cause-effect existence to possessing the very image of God and exhibiting why human beings are the crown of Creation.

One of the key ways we participate in human progress and demonstrate the fruit of a spiritually centered life is by a continuous refinement of this virtue we know as gentleness.

Anger has its place and its reasons. But gentleness is a higher power that takes us where anger never can.

SIX

I'm Taking Care of Me Right Now: SLOTH

"Stay away from the idiot instructor. I don't want you hanging out with him."

With these hurtful words, my childhood best friend's dad bestowed the title of "idiot instructor" on me. My friend's dad perceived that I was a slacker, a judgment all the more painful because he was partly right. He was convinced that I was not only an idiot in my lazy slacking behavior but that I had the power to turn other normal kids into idiots, and was therefore worthy of the title "idiot instructor."

My friend's father's complaint was that I was a sluggard. Although I cut grass, rode bikes, played ball, and did okay in school, the reality is that I was a very dejected young boy. It wasn't like I was some happy-go-lucky character like the Fonz, Fresh Prince, or Maynard G. Krebs. I wasn't a goof off. I was a young man with little hope, little self-worth, and even less motivation.

The truth is, I frankly didn't like my childhood a lot. I was an overweight kid who was clumsy and had trouble keeping up running and riding bicycles. I had a lot of fears about life, and especially bigger kids. I got teased and picked on enough to feel the pain of that sort of treatment. I began to believe that I was pretty much of a loser. I focused upon all that I could not do well and internalized every single feeling. I still remember feeling very lethargic and very unenthusiastic on a daily basis.

I was deeply depressed a good part of my childhood from about age eleven to age fifteen. I was growing like a weed. I was going through the usual adolescent body changes and I found it way more comforting to sleep than to face life. Thus, I slept a lot. My sleep and dreaming were not cures for natural exhaustion. They were escapes from emotional exhaustion. Escapes from the real world where I didn't feel as if I fit. Sleeping was painless. I didn't have to face my issues. I had little hope. I declared myself nonathletic material, noncollege material, and nonromantic material. And I slept. This is the insidious nature of sloth. Sloth is overly self-conscious, particularly of the negativity and deficiencies we all experience with ourselves.

I would go to school, do my work, come home, eat dinner, and then sleep until bedtime, then sleep some more until morning. My family and extended family teased me about it mercilessly. I became renowned for the ability to fall asleep on short notice in any location where I could lie down. I'd sleep at my grandparents, at friends' houses, at the drop of a hat. I would fall asleep nightly on the family couch in front of the television. The only time I felt good about me was when I didn't feel at all.

This pattern of escaping from a life I didn't like had some carryover. I responded dully and listlessly to most ideas. I gave up trying at school. And, since it was the sixties, I discovered marijuana, which for me amplified the dejection. Given the choice of being truly alive to God and to life, or being asleep, many more of us than you might expect would select the sleep state. I am personally convinced that many drug and alcohol habits are self-administered anesthetics. These substances kill the pain of consciousness, indeed obliterate consciousness itself to spare our human organism of the suffering we feel life holds for us. We sleep our way through life because reality is too stark, too painful, too demanding for us. If there is a laziness in sloth, an inactivity, then that inactivity is expressed in our unwillingness to change the way we view the world and subsequently the way we view ourselves. This laziness feathers a nest in which sloth can roost.

In the end, I created a condition of "sloth" in my character. It wasn't until late in my college career that, by God's grace, I woke up and decided to make something of my life. I still consider it a miracle. I didn't do it by myself. I was the victim of a conspiracy executed upon me by friends and teachers at my school. They believed in me when I couldn't believe in myself at all. Several teachers gave me constant support, looking for ways to spot and affirm gifts in me. Another gave me responsibilities. Yet another teacher got a job where I worked part time and rode to work with me to encourage me. He didn't really need the job. My friends would meet my negative self-image with, "You don't see what you have going for you." Eventually these positive forces plus the grace of God broke through in my life. I went from apathetic to passionate in a fairly short time and my life changed dramatically.

The fourth of the Seven Deadly Sins is "sloth." Sloth is not simple laziness. It is beyond idleness. Sloth is a personal state of dejectedness in mind and spirit. Sloth sucks the energy from the total person and leaves an existential sluggishness that makes one fearful, hesitant, weak-willed, and despairing. Sloth erases hope and amplifies despair.

Sloth is perhaps the most severe state of personal oppression that one can possibly experience. Sloth sounds like such a medieval word. Yet, in spite of its links to antiquity, it is a powerful problem today. Look at the pathologies of depression, anxiety, and despair that are rampant in modern society. I don't mean to say that all of these originate in or result in the sin of sloth. But I do think we should take a look at our lives, and see if any of the issue of sloth relates to us. Any down, depressing, or negative emotional state could be evidence of sloth. It's worth checking into. As I view sloth in my own life and in the lives of others, I notice that sloth starts slowly and builds over a long time. While anger, lust, and greed are explosive, sloth is intrusive. Sloth moves quietly into our lives and quietly builds an arsenal that destroys. Perfect sloth would lead a person to live unknown, make no contribution, and die unknown and unregarded. Sloth at its height renders one's life invisible.

One place I see sloth is in the rising nihilism inherent in postmodern culture and philosophy. Nihilism is a philosophical belief system stating that nothing in life can truly be understood, that nothing matters, that all human activity is a quest for the power to oppress others. It is the philosophy of "nothingness."

Any claim to objective truth is correctly suspect. One would think such suspicion would lead persons on a quest for truth. What really is true and what do I do about it? Instead, many of us gobble up the culture of cynicism in which we live and purchase shares of despair. Many of us view the challenges and problems of this world and make the ultimate statement of despondency: "What can one person do to change anything?" Sloth lies to us. Sloth attempts to convince us that we are powerless and that our lives don't matter.

The statements that "nothing matters" and "life cannot be figured out" are vast overstatements. We all know that things matter. We all have a scale of what matters most and least to us. But so often in our culture, probing and serious questions are answered with "Yeah" or "Whatever." Whether we are excited and enthused about what matters most or not, the fact is that we each do value certain things more than others. And to say that life cannot be figured out is to assume that there is no way anyone can live in reality and adapt to life. Sloth tells us a terrible lie: It tells us that there is no hope.

Sloth also encourages us to ignore those around us and focus on our personal misery. This is a travesty we commit against those who watch us practice sloth. I met a woman recently who was working hard to achieve a healthy adult life. She suffered from some serious hang-ups she developed in childhood. When I asked her to tell her story, she shared that her mother was despondent and nonresponsive. She tried to be the perfect kid and got no response. She reversed her strategy and tried to get in trouble in order to get attention and love from her mother. That didn't work either. Soon, this now-growing Christian woman accepted her mother's worldview and subsequent pathology. She gave up, too. After years of despondency and listlessness (sloth), she didn't know she could even have hopes or dreams, friends or family. With much prayer and the help of a skilled therapist and the support of Christian friends, this woman emerged from the dark fog of sloth. Her life is still lived cautiously and slowly, but not without hope.

Beyond the intellectual flaw of nihilistic philosophy of nothingness is the pleasure principle of hedonism—maximize pleasure, minimize pain. I actually have friends who claim this mode of thinking as their way of life. When held accountable for an action, they simply say, "It felt good," "It brought me pleasure," or, "It snuffed out the pain." And believe me, practical hedonism rules in our culture. We are all but begged to lie back, hang loose, slow down, and look out for "me."

Wallowing in the sorrows of sloth focuses us more and more on our self. We attempt to find a new source of meaning and purpose in ourselves. And frankly, psychological research shows again and again that the lonely self is a downright horrible place to find meaning. A deep descent into self is referred to in philosophical and ethical circles as egoism. Egoism, hedonism, and nihilism have similar roots and make powerful drivers at the controls of a human life. All of them place the entire meaning of life in the lonely self. Being overly self-referential causes us to ignore other important data—the lives of others and the sovereignty of God.

When sloth has its day, its victim says, "I'm okay just the way I am. I am just who I am." At this point of resignation, the person becomes less than a human person. Sloth has robbed him or her of dignity and a huge chunk of humanity. Sloth causes us to lose self-confidence and self-esteem. Sloth convinces us that there is no hope for change or progress. Sloth convinces us there is no reason to live. Why bother?

We bother because to be truly human is to be alive to life and continually growing. One of the early church fathers said, "The glory of God is the human person truly alive." Isn't that a great theological insight? God delights in human beings being fully human and developing toward their awesome potential with His help. Sloth sabotages God's process of making us whole and truly alive. Sloth lies to us saying that the mess we are is okay, and even if the mess we are wasn't okay, there's nothing we can do about it.

In addition to embodying a fundamental denial of God's rule over all of life, there is a rejection of the notion of personal destiny. In sloth we lose the notion that we are becoming "someone." And, in sloth we lose the notion that our life counts.

Perhaps even more dreadful, sloth indicates the abdication of responsibility by the person who succumbs to sloth. Taking responsibility for our lives is a must. Sloth is the ultimate denial. We have some issues that we need to deal with. Rather than think them through, we pour a tall Scotch, light a joint, turn on some inane television program, or take a nap. We feel like we're taking control when we take a little time for ourselves, pamper ourselves, and do things our way. And we love the sin of sloth just as we love all of the other deadly sins. But the crime we commit against our Creator and against ourselves is that our choice to be slothful is a choice made in bondage. The freedom we think we are practicing is actually a horrible bondage; a bondage that comes from abdicating our true responsibility to choose.

Now don't get me wrong. I am in no way advocating that we eliminate rest, renewal, recreation, and reflection from life. I often take naps. They aren't escapes. They are warm-ups to help me live the rest of the day with panache. Rest is essential. But rest, recreation, reflection, and renewal are intentional choices, made out of a responsible, accountable sense of self-management.

Sloth lacks the intentionality of these more wholesome cessations from activity. Sloth is a default mode of escape. Its purpose isn't to reenergize, learn from the past, or envision the future. Sloth's purpose is to black out the past, hold the future at bay, and, at all costs, avoid the present. Fighting this urge to escape is difficult. The retreat to a dark inner space seems so much safer than really trying to live life. Besides, if we hide away, maybe we will go unnoticed.

Pride and envy can easily be disguised. Anger is very public much of the time. Sloth is a private sin that we also think we can disguise. But while we fool ourselves, we don't do too well fooling others. Our sloth issues show through our despondent attitudes and a bias toward inaction.

Our rationalizations for sloth usually encroach upon the mercy of those around us. We tearfully recount how difficult and unfair our life is. We tell tales of woe about why we cannot cope and adapt to life. We solicit pity in order to get permission to remain idle. And our idleness becomes a sort of idolatry where we worship and exalt our self-manufactured misery to the level of "this is what life is."

Sloth is one of those nasty little sins that visit many of us in many different ways. We have really learned to put some fancy window-dressing on sloth. We make it look good and acceptable. Sloth can be rationalized as well as any other sin, and oh, are we good at it.

We might say that the evil in the world is too great to fight. Yeah, sure there are a lot of problems out there, but what is someone like me going to do about them? We denigrate the power of our life and the conviction of our voice while wrapping ourselves in the cocoon of sloth. Now our despair seems universal. We might even deceive ourselves and others into believing that the source of our dejection is just plain exhaustion from carrying the weight of the world on our shoulders. Many of us overestimate the cost of giving of ourselves and working to make a better world. I, too, often hear people saying that they are burned out from doing helpful ministries. Whenever I hear this statement about burnout, I immediately know that the person I am listening to is more likely in spiritual and emotional danger from retreating to sloth than he or she is prone to clinical burnout.

Fear is another cover for sloth. We say we are not comfortable with something right now. It buys us an escape to share with others that we have some fears that have haunted us and made it very difficult for us to get out there and really engage in life.

If you're like me, you can probably relate to another way to put a mask on sloth. I love this one. It's called playing the victim. My parents didn't raise me right. My first spouse neglected me. My employer didn't understand me. Once we declare ourselves the victim, we automatically claim the right to take any action we deem appropriate to bring relief to ourselves. It's a nasty little game we play with our own head. We convince ourselves that hiding out will make the bad things go away.

Another favorite camouflage for sloth is anxiety. I word-spin my latent depression and dejection into a "poor me" argument. My self-portrait of a perfect victim is based upon my high level of angst. My anxiousness begs others to pity me and handle me with kid gloves. My anxiety warns others to stay back and take it real easy with me. I meet people like this in churches all the time. They come to a Christian community wanting to be validated in their thoughts and beliefs—and they leave outraged when challenged.

The problem is that once we declare ourselves frail and anxious, we forbid others to come close or touch our lives. How could anyone dare speak strong words to me? Can't they see how fragile I am right now? I see this defense shield being used by many people on a daily basis. How often have I heard, "If you only knew what a hard time I have coping, you would feel sorry for me and you wouldn't be suggesting that I think about my life differently." The fact is, this person didn't want to view her life differently. Doing so would have made her accountable to do something with her life other than playing the retreating victim, the one with no reason to engage in real life.

I am not saying that depression, concern over world events, fear, and anxiety are not real. They are. If someone holds a gun in your face, go ahead and be afraid. If an earthquake kills thousands in Turkey, go with the pain. It's awful. If you have a biopsy for breast cancer or prostate cancer, give yourself permission to be anxious for a time.

But when we attach these strong emotions to sloth and use them to cover our core dejection, we are only making our sloth problem worse. We are burying it behind a mountain of excuses.

And speaking of excuses, here's the one I hate the most: "I am just taking some time for me right now." The assumptions inherent in that ten-word statement compose the greatest lie of all time. Taking time for me only turns us inward. Taking time for me places self rather than God at the center of the universe. Sloth is a increasingly discouraging journey inward; deep into our own dark and empty cave. Let me distinguish as carefully as possible the difference between wallowing in an inner mire of despondency and a more positive act of self-recognition. The first is an act designed to intensify misery and reinforce sloth's power to make us give up. The latter, self-recognition, has to do with courageously facing ourselves as we are, and working with God to live our destiny. Now, for those struggling with sloth, I recommend against starting with the inner issues. In fact, what we sloth sufferers need is a dose of focusing on what is outside of and around us. Battling sloth means not taking "a little time for me right now."

Again, am I being a little extreme? Don't we all take a little time for me? Sure we do. I love to read page-turner novels. I love to go to movies alone and relax. I love to kill time cruising on our boat. You probably have similar self-interested diversions. There is nothing wrong with any of these in proper doses. But sloth's motto is "I need time for me."

Eventually though, me is all there is time for—and as the self becomes more and more alienated, it also becomes more and more desolate. The end result is a twilight zone experience: a frightening world consisting of just one room, occupied by me alone, the walls steadily closing in.

As we become self-absorbed and the self loses definition, the very problems we are trying to understand amplify themselves. The abyss becomes deeper and deeper, the despair unrelenting.

Is there a way out of sloth? The idleness of sloth so easily overcomes one. You see, sloth is a sin of neglect. We neglect what is important for us. We neglect our calling and destiny. We neglect personal growth and personal health. We neglect God and spiritual progress. We neglect our neighbors. Sloth is the activity of no activity. And personal introspection cannot deliver us from the jaws of sloth; in fact, introspection only causes us to fall deeper into the pit of despair. If sloth is neglect of what is important, then it seems reasonable that attention to what has been neglected might provide a road to recovery. Attention to God. Attention to signs of hope. Attention to your spiritual gifts. Attention to the relationships that really matter in your life. And attention to the Bible that helps keep your vision focused on what is real.

In the midst of the neglect which is sloth, there develops a complex religion of the "self." This religion of the self rejects the one true God. In a sense, sloth declares all God's statements about life and meaning to be lies and asserts a new "truth" about life that is a distortion. This distortion gives you or me the opportunity to deepen our sloth by stewing in dejection, polluting our lives with fear and becoming immobilized by anxiety.

How can we free ourselves of such a hideous sin as sloth? Or if we can't be free of sloth, how can we work to keep it at a minimum? The best answer I can offer is the virtue of faithfulness. Faithfulness means to live, act, take responsibility for one's life and create something. Make things happen. Faithfulness is steady progress in doing the right things. It means keeping our nose to the grindstone. As I mentioned earlier, sloth is a sin we love which originates in neglect. If neglect is the problem, then proper attention is an antidote. Faithfulness is attentiveness. A very good friend of mine summarized his successful business enterprise when he said, "We say what we do, then we do what we say." Faithfulness. Steady plodding progress by paying attention to the little things.

One Old Testament wisdom saying is, "Little foxes spoil the vine." That's great imagery. Picture a vineyard, lush with vines, grape leaves, and grapes. It looks absolutely perfect. Unfortunately, near the roots of the vines, running under cover, small mammals chew at the very base of the vines rendering them dead well before any decay is seen in the vine, leaves, and grapes.

Sloth's activity is subtle. It comes from lies we tell ourselves about the way things are. Little lies. Tiny distortions. But each one gnaws at the very roots of who we are and who we are becoming. If little foxes spoil the vine, then we do well to pay attention to the little things if we are to countermand the effects of sloth. Faithfulness, a fruit of the Holy Spirit, actually energizes a love of the small things and a love for the long haul within us.

Industrious behavior is an expression of the spiritual fruit of faithfulness. Faithfulness shapes our lives. Long-term, steady commitment to living life to its fullest, fulfilling our obligations and reaching for our destiny, is what we are designed to do. We all want to be faithful to God, faithful in our relationships and faithful in our pursuit of vocation. The Apostle Paul gives some good advice to misdirected efforts when he says, "Let those who work eat" and "Let those who steal, stop stealing and do work that builds the common good." Paul's two-thousand-year-old call to faithfulness rings true for today. Each of us is accountable to take responsibility for our lives and do work that provides for our basic needs. We are not here to be taken care of. We are here to care for; for ourselves and others. Paul reminds us that we cannot live lives of sloth. We cannot live in isolation. We must work to provide for the common good. Our lives are important. We are linked. We are interdependent. Sloth sells us the illusion of independence and alienation. Something in us makes us anxious to buy sloth in huge quantities. Sloth makes a lie of safety and makes solitude sound like the truth.

For Aristotle, his number-two virtue was courage. Courage corresponds with faithfulness. Faithfulness calls for us to live beyond our fears, to live beyond our past and to do what is required of us today, irrespective of the challenges. Courage begs us to engage in real life, to become who we are becoming, own who we are and face what we must face—all for the long haul. Courage, like faithfulness, helps us stand tall and fight the good fight, whatever the day may hold. Courage is the commitment to never give up. A friend of mine is battling a life-threatening illness. He has undergone several very complex surgeries. Each time, he has faced his medical problem and his surgeries with an unusual courage: "They are going to fix it this time." Facing relapses, he says, "This time's the time we'll get it taken care of for good." He says, "With God's help, I can face anything and I can know for sure that all's well in the end. I have no reason not to stand tall and fight." This man is a hero of mine. I pray that someday I can express such sincere courage in the face of seemingly insurmountable odds.

It is interesting to me that there is so little debate about the value of faithfulness. Psychotherapists routinely prescribe exercise and community service to others as pathways out of despair, depression, and anxiety. They also prescribe a certain faithfulness about taking action on life issues. A well-known speaker on panic-anxiety disorder reports that you and I cannot get better until we own our feelings and recognize what is going on inside our bodies. The best way to attack our personal issues of fear, anxiousness, and despair is to recognize the issues and talk about them. This again is an act of faithfulness. It's hard work to delve deeply into the issues in our lives. There is much pain and sorrow. There is much to fear and loathe. There are some good reasons to deny and avoid the problems we all face. But faithfulness—a commitment to take all the steps one at a time—pays great dividends. Unfortunately, we who measure results on a daily basis become bored or frustrated with faithfulness because its sure growth is such slow growth. In a quick-fix world, waiting, watching, and measuring results by the year or perhaps the decade seem unthinkable. So, if faithfulness is the slow, steady hygiene for the soul pollution we know as sloth, then we must buy into the working of faithfulness for the long haul.

The therapeutic and spiritual concepts of courage, faithfulness, and industriousness are not at all out of line with teaching from the New Testament in which the Apostle Paul writes to first-century

Christians in Thessalonica, "I was not idle when I was with you and I did not fail to pay for my meals. My colleagues and I worked day and night to avoid putting you out. . . . Try not to alienate a person who is idle, but warn them of the deep personal peril they are facing."

Paul advocates for a faithfulness that reclaims responsibility for oneself. He offered in a parallel text that those who once stole should stop stealing and do something productive with their hands (their life). We mean something to each other. If we will move outside of ourselves and invest in others, we will over time see the fruits of faithfulness. And we will be thrilled.

I recently said a prayer of thanks for a man and a woman who have had a difficult time raising their son. They are wonderful loving people. They certainly aren't perfect. Their son was out of control. At one point in his middle teenage years, I figured I would spend the rest of my relationship with him by visiting him in a penitentiary. I am not exaggerating. This kid was on a path of destruction.

The parents never gave up. They remained positive, consistent, gracious, loving, and firm in their resolve to help shape a productive young adult. Their faithfulness and courage in the face of verbal and sometimes physical tirades paid off. After about four years of a living hell, the young man reversed his course in life. He finished school, got a job, assists handicapped adults, and is a joy to be around. His faith is alive and growing. While five years ago this young fellow met me with a sneer at church, he now approaches me intentionally, shakes my hand, and comments on my sermon or other aspects of worship.

The faithfulness of his parents. The courage of his parents. The help of the larger interdependent community created an opportunity for love to triumph. The sort of faithfulness we see in a model like these parents shows how steady and true faithfulness is.

These admonitions from Paul to be faithful and productive bear ancient wisdom, and their basic tenets of faithfulness are affirmed in the therapeutic community as well.

There is yet another level of faithfulness that I take very seriously. That is spiritual faithfulness. By this I mean, prayer, self-discovery, calling, and vision. Let me take a little time to flesh out each of these.

Spiritual faithfulness starts with prayer. Instead of pulling our head and heart into a shell, prayer opens us to the possibility that there is more than just us. It mystically connects us to God and begins reassuring us that we are not alone.

"This is the cosmos, and we are alone." I remember Carl Sagan's opening words to the PBS show *Cosmos*. As I sat in front of my television set years ago and listened to this pitiful pronouncement of the human condition, I would shudder.

". . . you are alone" echoed in my head, reverberating the final word, "alone, alone, alone, alone." This brilliant show functioned on the assumption that there was no God. I found so much of the program fascinating, but was also troubled by the dismissal of faith and the introduction of the idea of alienation. Several years ago, Sagan checked into a Seattle clinic for treatment of cancer. He had a bone marrow transplant. Tragically, the positive effects of the transplant did not last long. But during the short time that Sagan was well after the procedure, he reversed field on himself.

After careful thought, (and I think some prayer) during his illness, he came to the conclusion that his beliefs about the genesis and evolution of the universe did not in any way exclude the possibility of a transcendent, loving creator and sustainer of all that is. Sagan perhaps concluded life with a belief that proclaimed, "We are not alone."

We are not alone. God is with us. And prayer puts us in front of God. One of the great Christian thinkers of all time remarked that the first and foremost act of Christian obedience is "showing up in God's presence." The sixteenth century Reformers referred to this idea as *corum deo*. It literally means "in the face of God." To live a life worth living, it must be lived in the face of God. We cannot turn our backs on God. We cannot fix our eyes on the center of our soul in neglect of God. We are free to face God as loved and forgiven people. Prayer is the place where this Divine/Human connection begins.

Another critical step in spiritual faithfulness is self-discovery or self-recognition. Let me make some clarifying comments about self-discovery. It is a second step. The first step toward management of sloth is faithfulness in doing the little things. Take a walk. Shower. Clean house. Eat right. Sleep right. Give your best at work. Share yourself with your friends. Pray whether you sense God's presence or not.

But as we start a journey outward and away from the polluted core of our life, we must also be open to revisiting our inner places at such time as we feel strong enough. That time comes when we have sensed enough healing. The presence of God's Spirit within us fills our dark places with hope.

While working as a disc jockey a number of years ago, the station that employed me sponsored a Halloween haunted house. It was really, really scary. I don't much like scary events to begin with, but I had to work the promotion several nights. Interestingly, in the dark and cool of the night, I found the blood, gore, noises, and pouncing goblins way too much for me. But one day, I had to arrive at the haunted house earlier to do my show from there. I walked through the house in full daylight. I saw the little corners from whence ghouls jumped. I saw how the hangman's stunt worked. That which I had found ever so frightening was hardly of interest in the daylight. Further, my daylight tour took the fright out of the nighttime. I knew how everything worked.

When we have made enough progress in faithfully doing little things in our outer life, the Holy Spirit will cast a light on formerly dark places within us. This is the time where we are free to boldly ask ourselves what we fear, what makes us anxious, what we are gifted to do, what we are passionate about. This self-discovery process dictates that we stay present to ourselves in these times of searching in order to demand and answer, or at least, discern parts of the various answers. I am afraid Plato was right when he said, "The unexamined life is not worth living." An accurate assessment of our strengths and weaknesses, contributions we can make, and needs that we experience is essential for a life of growth.

Another aspect of spiritual faithfulness is developing a sense of calling. When most of us hear the word calling, we assume it refers to men or women called to be celibates, priests, missionaries, or pastors. And, yes, those are indeed valid callings. But the reality of calling is that each and every one of us was created by God for a purpose and we all have a calling. We have a destiny that we get to discover. Exploring and identifying our call is exhilarating. It is not always fun. We live behind this vale of tears called human life, where our world often fails to make sense. There is plenty of pain and sorrow. We wonder at times if God is really all-loving or even if God is there at all. There is a great deal of toil involved in most worthwhile pursuits. Yet, suffering the pain and frustration of identifying the call is at the heart of what it means to be truly alive and engaged. If sloth is due north, then discovering the call is as far south from sloth as one can go.

At a final level, spiritual faithfulness is about vision. The dejection of sloth blinds the eyes of the heart and vandalizes the artwork of the imagination. But vision opens us up again. Vision takes for granted that you and I are created for a purpose. It assumes that we know our strengths and limitations. It believes that we understand ourselves and our gifts and passions. Then, vision works to pull all of the elements of spiritual faithfulness into a synergistic bundle of meaning and purpose. Vision kindles possibilities in us. In the prophecy of Jeremiah in the Old Testament, God speaks to all humans, "I know the plans that I have for you. They are plans for good, not evil. They are plans of a future and a hope." God's plans come to us in vision.

Vision is the act of developing a clear and compelling picture of a desired future. Envisioning is working with God to cocreate a future full of goodness. Vision gives us something to live for and something to die for. Vision catalyzes the sense of longing for meaning and purpose that is latent in all of us and propels us into action. Practical faithfulness flows out of the vision that is a result of spiritual faithfulness. Sloth is inaction and all of these acts of faithfulness represent actions taken against sloth. Sloth is a lack of love. Calling and vision refire love within us. Love for God, love for self, love for others, love of truth.

Now, what makes this all so complicated is the interesting dynamics that take place in our lives when we face one particular sin, such as sloth. How often have we all experienced a formerly slothful person who becomes a self-made man. But when we hear the gutter-to-glory testimonies of someone like this selling their tape series or some other product, we don't always hear the fruit of the Spirit at work. Sometimes, we hear self-referential testimonies of people who think that they did it all by themselves.

I was recently dragged to a self-help guru's seminar in my town. I went under duress and I left when unguarded. What I experienced before I escaped was a man who laid it on thick about his days of sloth and what it was like for him to be totally down and out. Then, he proceeded to laud his newfound virtues, his wealth, and his belief that everyone could be just like him.

I am afraid that this poor chap might have inadvertently traded in his sloth for a double helping of pride. And don't disparage this man. Substituting one deadly sin for another is easy to do. They are all intrinsically interrelated. Each of the Seven Deadly Sins embodies a varying degree of the characteristics of the other six.

Even more insidious, sloth and all the other deadly sins have a strange payoff. They make us feel in control in the short term. And they seem to provide comfort and self-assurance.

The insidious nature of sin is that it is so remarkably attractive to most of us most of the time. Our calmer, more rational self wants what is right and good, but somehow we underperform as we are charmed, hypnotized, and deluded into believing that something as ugly and damaging as sin is somehow beautiful and acceptable. I guess that's why we refer to the Seven Deadly Sins as the sins we love.

SEVEN

It's Mine, Mine, Mine: GREED

We have interesting ways of expressing our sin of greed. One story that amuses me tells of a very wealthy old man who was desperately ill. He summoned his closest confidants to his bedside. Attending him were his doctor, his pastor, and his lawyer. You can probably imagine this solemn meeting of the minds.

The man said, "I know they say you can't take it with you, but who knows? What if the experts are mistaken? I want to account for all contingencies. So, I am giving each of you an envelope containing one hundred thousand dollars. When I die, I want you to each slip the envelope in my jacket pocket at the funeral service. Then, if I do need the money for the life to come, I will be ready. And I am giving the envelopes to you because you are my trusted and capable friends."

Soon enough, the old man did die. Each of his three advisers was seen slipping something into the deceased's coat pocket as he walked up to the open casket to pay his final respects.

Following the service, while the advisers were visiting with each other, the doctor displayed a sheepish look and said, "Fellas, I have a confession to make. You know with the cost of medicine today, I don't make all that much money. The hospital is desperate for funds. We can't even replace the CAT Scan machine that's broken down. So, I took twenty thousand dollars for the new CAT Scan and put the rest in the coffin."

The minister cleared his throat and looked down sheepishly at his shoe tops saying, "I, too, have a confession to make. As you know, our church is seriously overburdened by the needs of the homeless. I couldn't see just burying that money. So, in hopes of helping the homeless, I took fifty thousand dollars out of the envelope and put the rest in his pocket."

Fixing the doctor and minister with his gaze, the lawyer exclaimed, "I am astonished and deeply disappointed that you would treat our solemn trust so casually. He was our friend. I want you to know that I placed in his casket my personal check for the full one hundred thousand dollars."

This story is not a knock on lawyers. It could have been the butcher, the baker, and the candlestick maker. This is a jab at our tendency toward greed. We see something we want and it takes control of us. We act on our greed. We justify our greed. Greed is a desire to have more and more material comfort. Greed wants it all. Greed answers the question, "How much is enough?" by saying, "Nothing is ever enough."

Try this experiment with yourself. Ask "How much is enough for me?" Write it down, perhaps even in the margin of this page of this book. What came out on your list? I remember when I did my list during a summer study leave. I wanted a good marriage, a good relationship with my kids, a meaningful ministry that really makes a difference, decent health and longevity, good friends, a home, a boat. Now, here's what I experienced: No sooner had I completed the list with the belief that I did know what was enough, than I experienced an additional list of wants that swiftly became urgent needs. Having a house grew to a bigger and better house in a better neighborhood. My desire to have a boat grew to a bigger and newer boat. My desire for a meaningful ministry led me to ponder and desire a magnificent public ministry that would bring me acclaim.

As I have admitted my inability to call enough enough to others, I have listened to the stories of others as well. Many report that we share the same problem. Enough is not enough. We don't seem to have a good sense for when to call ourselves blessed. Instead, we seek more in a hungry, ugly foraging to feed our greed, believing that we are blessing ourselves.

The marvelous flaw in a greed mind-set is that if having it all is not enough, then we certainly cannot possibly consider giving any of what we have away. Rent one of the many filmed versions of Charles Dickens's *A Christmas Carol*. We laugh at Ebenezer Scrooge and his tightfisted ways. But our laughter is a little uncomfortable because we know that there's a bit of old Ebenezer in all of us. We hate to admit it because Scrooge is such a despicable man, and all of us want to be like the morally superior Bob Cratchett.

The historic name for greed that has often been attributed to the fifth of the Seven Deadly Sins is avarice. It covers the gamut of greed, miserliness, and stinginess. Each of these words expresses the insatiable desire to have and to hoard. Some people hoard money. Others hoard possessions. I have even seen this hoarding aspect of greed in people who are compulsive collectors. These poor folks have houses and garages full of items that are of little practical use. The value of these items is simply that they are possessed.

Avarice, or greed, is not the sin of having. To think of it this way leads to all sorts of trouble. I am the senior pastor of a growing church. I thank God for the high-asset people in our congregation. Wealthy people are stewards of resources that can help churches put God's radical love into action in our communities, particularly focusing on reducing the misery of the wounded and broken among us.

In one situation, an heir of one of the largest forest products companies in the world established a foundation that has been invaluable in founding a college, growing a major seminary, and undergirding the ministry of a major youth evangelism organization, as well as many other acts of Christian heroism.

Thank God for people who have. Frankly, I see many wealthy people whose everyday life utilizes a smaller percentage of their net worth than we middle-class wannabes who spend large sums to keep up with the Joneses. I denounce the pious saints who look down their nose at those whom God has blessed with extraordinary resources. I see these people mis-reading wealth for greed while pumping up their own level of pride.

Greed is not about having. Avarice is the sin of holding, possessing, and counting for the pure and simple fascination of saying, "mine." Avarice is a misuse of what we have. It can also be an inordinate desire to have what we don't have. The "mine" that lies at the center of greed is what twists a natural desire to be productive and take reasonable responsibility for our lives.

Greed can take shape in a number of materials, but money is the most frequent. I have numerous friends who have made mid-life career changes, confessing that the career of their youth was all about attaining power and titles that indicate success, and had very little to do with meaningful service to this world. Greed doesn't have to be just about money. Although, in an affluent society like ours, hoarding money evolves into possessing "stuff" for the sake of having it all. But money is a focal point.

Why money? Money is the material with which all material things are acquired and kept. Money is easy to count, easy to stack, and standardized in value. I have a philosophy about what money is and is not. It is a definition that goes beyond the simple definition of currency for mutual exchange. Money represents previously invested time units. If I make fifty dollars per hour at work and I spend fifteen hundred dollars per month for a house payment, then I am saying that my checking account directs the fruit of thirty hours of labor toward a monthly house payment. Similarly, if I live my life to God's glory and tithe off my four thousand-dollar-per-month salary, my four-hundred-dollar tithe represents eight hours, or one full day of work, done for the glory of God and the advancement of His kingdom. Money is how we keep score.

I live in Seattle, Washington. I recently learned that since 1985, Seattle has produced more millionaires than any other place in the world. Behind the windfall prosperity is a computer company whose two founders rank among the wealthiest men on earth. They possess the wealth of a small country each.

These industry leaders have been extraordinarily generous with their resources. What a blessing this has been. But while all this money is being made, I run into many who envy these new high-tech engineers and are pushing as hard as they can to accumulate similar amounts of money—not based upon need or opportunity, but based upon pure and simple greed. It's all about counting and keeping. It's about having for oneself, not for sharing.

Economics pioneer Adam Smith believed in the common good. While his seminal book *The Wealth of Nations* has been received as the manifesto for capitalism and personal gain, unfortunately, many remain confused about the philosophy of the deeply Christian Smith. He advocated for enlightened capitalism, which looks at the whole economy. Its goal is to create an increased common wealth which also results in individual wealth. Enlightened capitalism demands equity and justice. The entire nation must profit from our collective work. It's all about creating and sharing. Adam Smith said that this entire system was guided by an "invisible hand." In Smith's thinking, this invisible hand was clearly the loving, sovereign hand of God.

There have been times in our culture when I thought that this proper view of material goods was scoffed at. Perhaps you remember the movie *Wall Street*, which remains a popular video rental. The villain of the story, Gordon Gecko, announces at a meeting, "I don't produce. I don't create. I own." To own for the sake of owning is greed. Greed doesn't produce or create. It owns. And on the downside, when our greed kicks in to own, those whom we exclude from our personal blessings become victims of our greed. This disrupts the rhythm of life as it is meant to be.

Greed drastically reduces our contact with God. Who needs to say, "In God we trust" when we believe our good fortune is purely the result of our own accomplishments? Now, don't get me wrong. I don't object to hard work and good pay. In fact, I feel that good pay for the talents we share is a noble aspiration of any working person. I think the place where we fall down in Western culture is that we have obliterated the line between wants and needs. We have so much that we don't really know the difference between wants and needs. Providing for a family's needs and working hard to get that is not greedy. Unfortunately, most of us are of the mind-set that our list of needs includes international travel, ski boats, beach cottages, boats, etc.

"Fool. Tonight your life is going to be taken from you. What good does it do to have it all and lose your very soul?" Jesus uses these words in a story about a farmer who built huge barns to store all his valuable harvested grains. Moving from our Lord to the world of comedy, I once heard caustic comedienne Phyllis Diller say, "I've never seen an armored car following a hearse to a cemetery."

God gets to be God no matter what we say or do. As God's creatures, none of us is impervious to God's influence in our world or

His rightful claim upon our lives. We are not moral free agents. We don't proclaim goodness upon our own actions.

I once visited a man who claimed to be a Christian. He was pretty wealthy and had several very good and upstanding adult children. During a discussion of estate planning, he revealed that he refused to give annual cash gifts to his children in order to help them avoid estate taxes. He went on to justify his actions, saying, "I've been a great father to them already. I don't need to do that for them as well." As I scratched below the surface of this man's comments, I discovered an errant way of thinking. He was worried about his tens of thousands in spite of his multiple millions. The reasons for his tightness with his resources came down to his feeling that the money was his and he could make the calls—whether it seemed wasteful or caused hardship for others. He didn't care how much went to taxes.

At an even deeper level was a failure to recognize his own mortality and his need to trust God for all things, including financial resources. He felt the need to hoard his money until the day he died, imagining that the last day of his life might be farther off than his ample resources could reach. He failed to trust God.

When we fail to trust God to be God and take care of our daily bread, we step onto thin ice. Greed proclaims that God is not our provider, but rather we must exercise a supreme effort to get for ourselves what God cannot or might not provide. We claim the right to take care of ourselves and we set the rules of engagement. We say God helps them who help themselves and we then help ourselves to whatever we want. Greed causes us to establish our degrees of entitlement. We will offer ourselves what we think we deserve, no more and no less. Interestingly, the entitlement mentality plays into several of the sins we love. Entitlement makes us the justifiably needy recipient of whatever we feel we deserve whether it is reputation, venting of rage, hoarding, consuming, or sex outside of marriage. Entitlement thinking can really make a mess of our thought processes.

In the end, greed is a very serious misunderstanding of the true nature of things. You see, nothing that we have is ours. Everything is a gift from God. Everything we have is on loan; we are merely stewards. This is the reality of all things in this material world regardless of how we might assert a different truth.

Stewardship is an interesting concept. The word stewardship comes from the old English word, "sty ward." The sty ward was the person who looked after a farmer's pig sty. Over the centuries, the idea of being a worthy and reliable hireling has taken on some new twists, but the essential meaning is unchanged. Stewardship is the act of taking responsible care of what belongs to someone else.

I do some teaching for a local university and I enjoy being with young people a lot. One day during a break in a business ethics class, Dale came up to me and asked, "Dr. Rowland, is there any way I could borrow your car to take my new girlfriend out on a date?"

I agreed saying, "Treat it like it's your own."

The next day I got my car back. It was fueled up, washed, vacuumed, and spotless. I felt like asking my young friend if he'd like to use my car about once a week. The car he gave back to me was in better shape than the car I gave to him.

What would have happened had Dale not been such a good steward? Imagine my car filthy dirty with a huge pile of fast-food trash on the floors, out of fuel. Would I ever loan Dale a car again? No way.

Stewardship is taking care of something that belongs to someone else and giving it back to them in as good or better condition than when we received it.

Isn't that a great picture for our lives? Instead of thinking that we are entitled to "all" with no regard to God or others, we can actually take what is given to us by God and use it skillfully to create value in this world. I have often observed that truly alive human beings create value wherever they go. They make others feel important. They enrich lives. They usher goodness into a broken world. You and I have the opportunity to create abundance and value in our world. Holding us back from that noble aspiration is the deadly sin of greed.

As a pastor of a church, one of the hardest things I have to talk about is the finances of the church and the entire issue of tithing. Amazingly, as hard as it is to convince people to try tithing, I have never heard someone say, "We tried tithing faithfully; it hurt us financially and we had to stop or go bankrupt." More often I hear, "We are trying tithing and it's fun. God is taking care of us. We really do have more discipline and order in our financial life." In fact, people who take the first risk to give very often wind up giving a greater amount in succeeding years simply because of the joy that giving brings. These are the people who are blessed. They give of themselves and watch others grow as children are nurtured in a good ministry, adolescents are evangelized by Young Life, and homeless adults are ministered to at the local missions. When we give, we become intrinsically involved in our community—and we receive the incredible gift of delighting in the difference we are able to help create in our world.

We don't live to accumulate. We live to love, share, and generate goodness. We can do that as poor persons, as middle-class persons, or as extremely rich persons, unless we fall prey to the deceitfulness of avarice.

Frequently, I see a bumper sticker that says, "Whoever who has the most toys when he dies wins." There is a great pressure on us to accumulate, to compete, to get ahead, to have the most. We get lured into success and gain ever so easily.

Our upward, grasping maneuvers lead us to posture and pose, to move into homogeneous, gated communities where people are more "our type of folks." We build perfect homes with perfect carpets upon which no one is allowed to tread. And in the end the miserly are alone, empty and unfulfilled because having a lot is not good enough. We must have it all when we accept avarice as a life partner.

Money is not bad. But the love of money is a powerful force that can corrupt us terribly. Money can become an evil idol if misunderstood and wrongly utilized.

Several years ago, Peter, an eighteen-year-old from Dublin, Ireland, came to live with our family. We love this talented young musician. One day Peter and I were standing in line to pay admission to a matinee movie.

We had been talking about Irish culture and American culture, so in jest I showed him a dollar bill and said, "It should be obvious that America is a Christian country. I mean look, right here it says, 'In God we trust.' "

Peter hardly paused before pointing at the dollar bill and saying, "Yeah, but that *is* your god." I wish he was wrong, but I don't think Peter's observation can be disregarded.

The classical picture of avarice is a part of Dante's *Inferno*. In the *Inferno*, residents of Hell are being punished for the deadly sins that characterized their runaway lives. The picture drawn for greed is an image of a person in Hell with his head pushed down into the dirt with a caption saying, "I have turned my back on heaven." Turning our backs on heaven because we treasure the material things of earth is a distortion of love, an improper placement of love. Greed is too much love for things that don't matter all that much and too little love for the things that really do matter.

I met an unfortunate man in a congregation where I once served. This fellow was very wealthy. He owned several businesses, three homes, seven cars, a few boats, and every imaginable toy, buttressed by substantial investment accounts.

He said, "I want to love, serve, and honor God and also desire to serve and support my family." But he couldn't seem to bring himself to the place where he would like to be. Instead, he buzz-sawed through marriages, was stingy with his numerous kids, and was a desolate, miserable soul.

During my association with this man, I had the misfortune of seeing his annual pledge to the church. It was twenty-five dollars, paid in cash on the thirtieth of December each year. Now while it is true that this man may have given finances to charitable organizations other than the local church, his twenty-five dollars didn't do much to affirm his desire to honor God within that congregation. What a sad story—someone fully capable of being generous chooses instead to suffocate in his own greed. I really like this man, and yet I pity him. He just doesn't get it. His tightfistedness may be rooted in fear or insecurity, but when all is said and done, he's just a miser. And he's lonely and miserable to boot.

My mentor, Bruce Larson, tells a story about a wealthy man who came into his office when he pastored a Seattle church. Bruce had been speaking about tithing, saying that the first way to get yourself freed up and properly prioritized is to give 10 percent of what you make to God's kingdom as an act of faith and love. Bruce even cited research from the field of psychology that demonstrated that people who are givers are happier, live longer, and manage money more responsibly.

During Bruce's conversation with the rich church member, the man said, "You've been talking a lot about tithing. I am definitely listening and growing as a Christian, but Bruce, I make a ton of money. I can't possibly tithe. That would be a huge hunk of cash."

Bruce, in his wisdom, asked the man if he wanted to pray about it. The man agreed and opened an out loud prayer by asking for God's guidance in the matter of giving. Bruce prayed next, "God, help my dear brother here earn less money this coming year so that he can afford to tithe."

Miserly, stingy behavior is capable of mustering fantastic rationalizations. Imagine. I can't give because I have too much. This conclusion seems preposterous to those of us reading this story, yet in our own ways we affirm greed as a sin we love and we develop our own excuses for our sinful behavior.

The word "miser" is derived from the same root word from which we derive the word "misery." A miser is a miserable person. The source of the misery is the distraction from what is real, good, important, and honorable.

Distraction comes from the Latin word *distractus*, which actually means "to be torn apart." Avarice distracts us from what is real and true and important. Greed distorts our concept of reality and eventually convinces us to believe the lie that we must have and hold on to everything that we can get our hands on. Greed has such an intoxicating effect that there is little reasoning with a sufferer. We offer ideas of sharing, or otherwise breaking the cycle of greed, and our words are met with anger and defensiveness. Or perhaps, with a so-what sort of shrug. To the greed-intoxicated person, nothing other than greed makes any sense at all.

In the midst of the distraction and confusion caused by the intoxicant known as avarice, we lose track of some important things.

First of all, we lose track of the value of the things we hoard. We lessen their value. Money is no longer a representation of previously spent time; instead it is a devalued quantity. I cease to say, "Thank God for my work and all that you have blessed me with to live this life of mine and live for others as well." It doesn't make any difference if you have a philosophy about the nature of money. All that matters is how much one has and how much one must still acquire. The money no longer counts for anything valid. It is a pile of paper, good only for counting.

Second, distraction places all attention on the hoarded object. Instead of viewing the asset in its normal utility as a tool for the living of life, it is seen as the life itself. The asset is counted and stored, but never used to its fullest, therefore devaluing it. If money is best used when it is partially dedicated to the needy and to God's purposes, then the distraction of greed takes our eyes off worthy objects of our resources and focuses us on the money itself. Money's use is polluted. Money becomes a source of our alienation, paranoia, and our personal ascent to power.

Third, the intoxication of greed causes us to ignore and devalue the important people and things in life, including God, the giver of all good things. Have you ever purchased a gift for someone and received no thank you or acknowledgment whatsoever? It hurts, doesn't it? To know that you went out of your way to be gracious to someone and they totally ignored your generosity is painful. Avarice puts us at risk of failing to show gratitude to God and those around us.

Avarice puts us in a place where we ignore or keep something from the people we say we love. A true miser must spread his or her desire to hoard as widely as possible. Family and friends are invited into their pathology. Needs and wants of those who are close to the stingy person are ignored under the slogan, "It's mine. Get your own."

I would bet that just about all of us struggle with some form of greed. To be honest, a lot of the seemingly dumb stuff we do is rooted in some pretty good reasons. I know numerous misers who grew up during the Great Depression. My own father is an example. At the depths of the downturn in the 1930s, he and my grandpa were down to two pairs of shoes between them. One pair was pretty worn. They would rotate shoes to share the misery.

It's not hard to understand that someone who grew up in the midst of such economic strain would become an accumulator out of the fear of being poor again. I really do understand this motivation for stinginess and tightwad behavior. I think God understands it, too. That still doesn't make it right. As one of my friends often says, there are always lots of excuses, but excuses aren't reasons. We can excuse someone adapting to life with a miserly approach after being a victim of the Depression. But we cannot condone the behavior as a legitimate reason for welcoming a dangerous sin into our lives.

Others of us rationalize our miserliness by blaming parents. Our whole lives are lived trying to prove them wrong, exceed their own lifestyle accouterments, and thus declare ourselves valid. Okay, so some of us had less than perfect parents. But reacting with avarice doesn't bring us life—it alienates and destroys us at the core.

Still others will cite childhood abuses, snubs, or even handicaps and disabilities to justify a miserly approach to life. Again, those who listen to these people's personal stories, and even God, pity these folks for what they have gone through. But past history doesn't justify a habitual routine that results in a ruined life. This is true for all of the sins we love.

Breaking the habit of avarice is like breaking the habit of crack cocaine. I have ministered to a number of people trying to get off crack. It's scary because the withdrawal symptoms are severe and massive. Apparently the receptor center in the brain where crack goes to work becomes so addicted to the "hit" of the drug that it cannot live without it. The body and brain scream against the deprivation of not smoking more crack. Sadly, crack smokers often die using the drug or take their own lives because they cannot stand the pain of getting clean.

Avarice has the same cracklike power. Greed grips the inner essence of its victims and claims them for all eternity. Greed sends statements to its victims that they are becoming free—dependent upon no one, superior to everyone, and accountable to no one, even God. At the same time, while we are not looking, greed is sucking the life out of us—we don't see it because we are too busy listening to the lies avarice tells us.

Countermanding avarice is no easy task. Perhaps you remember the stories told of ancient mariners and sirens. Sirens were mythological mermaidlike creatures described as beings of awesome beauty possessing singing voices which were hypnotic. Mythology tells us that a sailor who listened to the voice or looked in the eyes of a siren would become mesmerized, jump in the water, and swim to her only to find an ugly sea monster whose singing voice was actually the banshee scream of a beast devouring human flesh.

How do we buffer ourselves against the banshee scream of greed?

As with all the Seven Deadly Sins, treating them and keeping them in check is accomplished only by continuous readjustments of attitudes, beliefs, and behaviors over a long, steady period of time. New habits that truly gain the power to expunge old habits are not easily cultured. Habits come from a combination of knowledge, desire, and skills.

Aristotle listed great-spiritedness as one of his seven virtues. This is the virtue of the open mind. An open mind wants to understand the world as it really is. Being open-minded enough to see the larger picture of life makes greed hard to justify.

Great-spiritedness is quick to say, "I don't know it all." In its quest for truth and righteousness, great-spiritedness opens one to the possibility of a "better way" to think and live. New knowledge alerts us to new ways of answering the questions, "What do I do and why should I do it?"

But knowledge alone won't get it done. We cannot live from our heads. We must have a passion in our hearts to do what is right. We have to want to become the people God intends us to be. It's all about desire. Without desire, knowledge is folly.

Before knowledge and desire can successfully be deployed, we must also have skills. Skills are the how-to side of behavioral change. Disciplines like regular, sacrificial giving to worthy causes develop liberality and generosity. Taking human relations courses or reading books may help develop skills in anger management, building self-esteem, and getting out of a mind-set of despair. Combined with knowledge and a fire in the belly that says, "I want to," skills lead us toward our goals.

The two virtues on which I would like to focus as long-term corrections for greed are peace and goodness. These two virtues are a part of the Apostle Paul's list of virtues representing the fruit of the Spirit that we will explore in depth in our closing chapter. Peace is the abiding sense that we are in God's hands and all is well. We needn't strive. Goodness stirs within us a desire to share who we are and what we have with others.

I mentioned earlier that distraction was a huge part of avarice. In fact, if you look at each of the Seven Deadly Sins, you will find distraction and self-centeredness as active agents in every sin. If being distracted is true to its Latin root meaning "torn apart," peace, which can also be translated as "wholeness," is the virtue that repairs the tear in the fabric of our souls.

Peace is a sense of everything being whole, in its right place and in its proper priority. Peace feels wonderful. It replaces the strain of being torn apart. Peace allows us to disengage from the menacing distractions that snare us and look at God, life, and ourselves in a new way. When we experience the God of peace, we want to live in God's peace. We desire to harmonize with God and others. Our rugged individualism begins to melt away in favor of a more community-focused understanding of life. At this point, how much I have is not nearly as important as ascertaining how "we" are all doing.

To be centered in peace is to be centered in God. The joy of our relationship with the Creator brings love—the satisfaction of longings and the fulfillment of desires—assurance amid our hopes and fears.

Those who find peace with God and in God discover that the secret of life has little to do with what we have. The secret of life is all about "who we have." Or, in God's case, who has us.

Attaining peace begins by intentionally quieting our minds, steadying our breathing, sitting still (even if uncomfortably still) in the presence of Almighty God and saying, "I'm here. What's up?"

There is no shortcut to inner peace. It starts in the presence of God, it moves to contemplation of the character of God, it adds contemplation on the real nature of life, and finishes with self-discovery and new strategies for living.

By the way, don't take peace as a passive, wimpy word. It's not. It is brilliantly powerful. Peace, as I defined earlier, means to have everything in its right place, being used toward its right purpose.

Our American understanding of peace is a cessation of tension. This is a faulty understanding. Let me share an example you might enjoy, especially if you are a water dog like me.

Sailboats are equipped with numerous sails for different purposes. Unused sails are stored in a sail locker in a nylon sail bag.
Stored sails have ceased their striving, but are they at peace? I
don't think so. What they really are is discarded lumps of fabric.

A sail is at peace when it is unfurled, trimmed by the winch,
and stretched to its maximum by a turn into the wind. Every grom-
met and rope on that sail is being yanked at magnum force. The material of the sail strains as it meets its destiny.

A good sail, well deployed, is a vision of peace. It possesses
beauty in spite of the savage forces pulling it at every corner. Its
beauty comes from its wholeness and purpose. Think about it.
When did you ever look out on the water at a colorful spinnaker on
a fast-moving sailboat and say, "Oh that poor thing, just look at the
stress it's under being pulled from all directions." What we usually
think is, "Wow! That's beautiful."

It is when we tune our lives to wholeness and purpose that we
really begin to live and find peace in living fully, as we were created
to do. The great thing is that this peace can be self-replenishing.
The more inner peace we experience, the more we want it for ourselves and for others.

Experiencing a growing sense of peace opens us to the possibility of goodness. Goodness is Paul's counterpart to Aristotle's
righteousness.

What Paul means by goodness, and what Aristotle means by
righteousness, is to be attuned to justice and all things that are
"right" and to act in harmony with those things. Goodness is found
in response to a natural disaster such as a tornado. Goodness is so
quick to send some money or board a plane to be a volunteer relief
worker that goodness never stops to ask, "Is this a good investment
for me?"

I still remember a stunning story about Peter Lynch, the origi-
nator of the Fidelity Magellan Fund, perhaps the most popular mu-

tual fund in history. Lynch was a Wall Street master. But he announced a surprising turn in his life when at age forty-eight, he retired.

Lynch said, "My father died young. I don't want to die at my desk." He was then asked what he was going to do. Many thought he would announce becoming a consultant.

Instead he said he was going to work in his church with kids: "Kids are a great investment. They beat the hell out of stocks."

Lynch's knowledge of life, his passion for the good, and his desire to build skills to reach kids put investing on a whole new level. Most of us think of investing as "What do I get out of it?" But a more enlightened form of investing—that done out of a spirit of goodness or righteousness—asks, "How can I invest in the common good?"

Aristotle viewed this investment in the common good as liberality. Interestingly, Aristotle did not denounce wealth. In fact, he said that part of liberality was spending rightly on fine objects. Some of those fine objects might be our own, but in Lynch's case, he discovered a new group of fine objects called America's youth. Suddenly valuing others places a new value on one's time and treasures.

To learn goodness, or what Aristotle refers to as liberality, is to realize that all good things, even our assets, come from God. In worship, we often sing "Praise God from whom all blessings flow . . ." Truer words have never been sung. Goodness causes us to focus on the Giver and accept what we have as "on-loan" assets, checked out from the library of heaven itself for the re-creation of a fallen world.

Interestingly enough, the turn from avarice to peace and goodness often results in liberality—in giving. And when we give, we discover that it is our destiny. Giving builds a fire inside our souls.

A former seminary professor of mine once said something that I cannot quote perfectly, but it goes something like this: "Birds have feet and can walk. Birds have talons and can grasp a branch securely. They can walk. They can cling. But flying is their characteristic action, and not until they are flying are they at their best. . . . Giving is what we do best. It is the air to which we were born. It is the action designed in us before birth and by our very nature."

Doesn't that absolutely inspire you? Isn't there something deep inside you that rises up to that vision of peace, purpose, goodness, and liberality? Every molecule in me screams, "Yes! That's what I want to do." Armed with the tools of peace and goodness, we can take captive the enemy of greed.

EIGHT

I Want It All and
I Want It Now:
GLUTTONY

From philosophers to psychologists to spiritual directors, numerous researchers of the human condition have noted that there are only two real fears in this world: the fear of living and the fear of dying. We are all inclined toward one or the other, except for those fortunate ones among us who suffer from both. The fear of living and the fear of dying both stimulate a similar response: the urge to consume. Consumerism is the modern-day manifestation of gluttony. Spiritual directors tell us that gluttony is an excessive amount of love for consuming things from food and beverages to other addictive behaviors including excessive shopping and collecting.

I don't know if you find yourself living under an illusion that sometimes captures me. It is the illusion that I can do everything I imagine in the lifetime I am given. I fantasize that I can do it all: cruise the world, write ten books, go to all of my favorite sporting events.

This "I can do it all" mentality sometimes allows me to behave very shortsightedly. Maybe you can relate to this, too. For instance, I want to lose weight and be healthy, but I want to eat everything I like in whatever quantity satisfies me. Gluttony focuses us on instant fulfillment of our most pressing, urgent, and immediately perceived need. Gluttony actually causes us to work at cross-purposes with ourselves.

"Eat, drink, and be merry, for tomorrow we die" is a sentiment that is suited to both the fear of living and the fear of dying. Our fear of living tells us to hide out with people we know in a small and comfortable world of our own making. It keeps us from making decisions and taking risks, thus preventing us from grasping the richness and abundance of a full life. Our fear of death urges us to grab all the gusto now, because if we have it all and do it all, we just might dodge the Grim Reaper, or, at least, won't have missed much when he comes to take us away. Besides, if we are going to die tomorrow, then the consequences of today's actions won't matter.

Led Zeppelin's famous song "Stairway to Heaven" is about a person who used consumerism in an attempt to purchase immortality. The famous words ring out, "and she's buying a stairway to heaven." Nice idea. No such luck. We cannot buy, eat or drink, collect, or shop our way to heaven. The only known agency providing eternal life is God Himself by the power that raised Our Lord Jesus from the dead.

Some of the great wisdom of the ages is printed on colorful posters and bumper stickers. I have seen many that poke fun at the fears that drive us and at how we use them to compensate in life. One such poster reflecting the fear of dying reads, "God put me here for a purpose, I cannot die until my work is done. At this point, I am so far behind that I am going to live forever." A cute little indication that we can easily cling to the earth and hope to justify our lives by filling them with work, food, booze, adventures, and relationships.

When left unchecked, the fear of living and the fear of dying cause us to react to life, rather than interact with life. In this reactive state, a vice known as gluttony is prone to occur. In fact, let's just call gluttony what it is: a sin we love. The grasping, consuming mentality that is gluttony dulls the pain of facing our fears and gives us a false sense of comfort.

A classic form of this fear- and pain-reducing role that gluttony plays is comfort food. When you and I are a little blue, to which cupboard, refrigerator shelf, fast-food store, or ice cream shop do we retreat to provide succor for our troubled souls? It is undeniable that gluttony is very much linked to the whole idea of needing to be comfortable now. We treat ourselves to gluttonous indulgences assuming we are helping ourselves, when actually we are issuing ourselves a death warrant by way of one of the Seven Deadly Sins.

Most of us think of gluttony as the sin of overeating or perhaps drinking too much. It is that, and more. Gluttony has to do with hanging on to the earth. Our fear of living, dying, or both causes us to clutch and consume, to make radical attempts at control. Have you ever had the feeling that you want to do and see everything before you die? This fantasy implies that we are going to live longer than we probably will and assumes that we have the capacity to do what no one else has done.

Think of Jesus. He lived thirty-three years. He never traveled more than a hundred miles from his birthplace. Yet, he remains the most celebrated and written about character in human history. None of us can do it all or have it all, and it certainly cannot all be done *now*. Gluttony is a little like greed, but there are also distinct differences.

While greed motivates us to hoard and hold, gluttony bids us to attack and consume. We hold on to the earth with such fervor that nothing else seems to matter. Conspicuous consumption. Now, do you think this flaw in the human condition that is cataloged as the sixth of the Seven Deadly Sins has any relevance for today? I do.

Yet, we take gluttony ever so lightly. We joke about our eating habits and the other ways we consume. Our cars bear bumper stickers that read "Born to Shop" or "When the going gets tough, the tough go shopping." On the other hand, we might take gluttony more seriously but attribute it only to persons with chronic eating or drinking disorders, giving little or no attention to our own propensity for gluttony through other forms of conspicuous consumption. I believe the reality of gluttony hits so close to home, most of us don't want to face it.

If you are like me, you want to make excuses for your excesses. I have been working really hard lately and I thought it would be good to spend some of my earnings on this or that. You might think of things you consume as little favors or rewards you give yourself in exchange for efforts and accomplishments in your life. It certainly isn't wrong to break away from routines, celebrate successes, or reward diligence. Don't get me wrong; these things can be good. What's so deceptive about gluttony is that we often fail to recognize the delineation between healthy and unhealthy consumption. This confusion inside all of us has actually predominated our contemporary culture.

During the 1980s, the rise in young, urban professionals created a subculture that became the ruling order of the day. Their motto was to have it all, do it all, and by all means make it happen now. One joking commentator called the yuppie era the age of "transcendental acquisition." My wife and I were walking to dinner one night behind some young adults all clad in black. A couple with three small children and a very yuppie look passed us going the other way. Seconds later, I overheard one of the young folks in front of us: "Good heavens! More yuppie larvae."

One Generation X (born 1965–83) complaint about baby boomers (born 1945–64) is that the boomers are a generation of conspicuous consumption. I think they rightly assess a weakness of the boomer generation. What they see in me (I am a boomer) is a desire to experience everything life has to offer without any regard to a set of priorities that makes life worth living.

Generation X, though mostly accurate in its critique of the boomers, is not immune to gluttony. This young and promising generation appears to be more focused upon the consumption of experiences than the boomers. Life's meaning is derived in having done it all—from extreme sports to world travel. Of course, like the American Dream of the World War II prosperity generation and the radical individualism and materialism of the baby boomer generation, Gen X'ers have their own expressions of gluttony, the sixth deadly sin.

While greed creates an environment of misery by hoarding and being stingy, gluttony is characterized by the desire to consume. A miser holds a modest party and keeps everyone in one room. When the food is gone the party is over. The miser is almost outside of his own party, watching and hoping that nothing is taken away from him. A practicing glutton attends her own party and screams, "Have another drink on me! The bar's open. There's tons of food and we're going to eat all night and party all night." The embarrassing part for me is that I am such a willing participant in this mind-set. There's nothing more humiliating than being lured into buying something by my latent gluttony only to realize I really didn't need or want it, nor do I have a place to put it!

I remember a recent trip to one of the chain stores that has it all. Because they had men's clothing, I bought some stuff. It was there. It was advertised. I am a fool. I have never worn the stuff and never will. I walk away from experiences like this feeling more like a king salmon than a human being. King salmon instinctively hit certain colored lures at certain times of the year. They don't think, they just bite, and wind up filleted.

Gluttony causes us to bite on a flash. We take whatever color lure is presented to us and we wind up—body, soul, and mind—in the frying pan. It's humiliating, isn't it?

I know that I am not alone. I have read much and have done graduate studies in marketing research and consumer behavior. The fact is that there are many of us who are not very discriminating shoppers and consumers. Most of us snap at the flash of the right lure by eating, drinking, spending, buying, or indulging ourselves in some other way. And if you don't think the Madison Avenue types in marketing and advertising know this about us, you are sorely mistaken.

Researchers test commercials on "typical" volunteer consumers. By testing skin moisture, blood pressure, heart rate, and pupil dilation, the marketing and advertising researchers can tell which images spark the primal, nonrational response that precedes a "buy decision."

Most of us are programmed to respond to certain images unconsciously. Now, I don't want to excuse the acts of consumption and deny their sinfulness under the guise that they are nonrational or subconscious. You and I are responsible for the messages to which we expose ourselves. And, we are responsible for how we process the messages we receive. In every sense, when we allow our culture to make gluttons of us, we have ourselves and no one else to blame. Worse than believing outright lies about consumption, we allow our flawed and broken humanity to distort good, positive images and submit to calls for consumption. Perhaps some of the programming is actually a gift of God to His human creatures. For instance, over 97 percent of all women's heart rates increase and their eyes dilate upon seeing a baby. Maybe God put that response in women as part of the mothering instinct to ensure that helpless infants would survive. Now, combine that cute little baby face with a marketer's demand to buy all the baby toys and equipment imaginable and a lovely, natural instinct is polluted. A caring person who lets a natural instinct become distorted by negative messages from Madison Avenue becomes a habitual consumer, mistakenly thinking that her gluttony is really a drive to nurture her child. Amazing. The sin of gluttony is a sin we love, because it panders to the distortions within us.

Men have a similar response to women that women have to babies. Add a beautiful face, long legs, shapely breasts, or a well-shaped posterior to any advertising message appealing to men and they experience dilated eyes, increased blood pressure, rising heart rate, and moistening of the skin. This makes men open to the product being sold.

The male response to female beauty is part of men's God-given attraction to the looks of the opposite sex. Built into men is a desire to cherish and adore the woman of their dreams. The male response desires fulfillment in intimacy and responsible family life. But pollution again sets in.

The female image is used in advertising with intentional focus upon physical attributes that arouse sexual interest and products are often sold on the erroneous notion that if we men purchase a product, women will flock to us seeking sexual adventure. We somehow think the product being sold to us will bring us satisfaction, but it won't. In one magazine ad for a popular cologne, a couple sits naked in a tire swing. The advertisement's message is clear—use this cologne and you'll have a sexual adventure in a tire swing. One comedian joked about this ad: "I have bought bottles and bottles of this stuff. I have my tire swing up and my clothes off. But I'm alone and cold. I don't know if this stuff works or not." In this case, the ad sells an image of sex that is less than honorable and tempts us to attain it by the use of the cologne. It can also go the other way around. Let's say I want to be a good provider for my family. My goal is my family's welfare. Ads come on the television telling me that a good father buys his kid a certain product. My goal of being a good father is compromised at this point. My internal dissonance says to me, "Buy. Consume. Be a good dad." Or, "Hold off and be a bad dad." In short order my goal of being a good dad is displaced and the distortion that I must give in to the screaming voice of gluttony has me thinking "I must have this. I must consume it."

Take a look at beer ads in particular. Bikini-clad sex symbols jump in and help carry the cooler of brews down to the beach with the implication of "if you've got beer, you've got us." It seems so silly, but it works. On the whole, this method has been more successful than animated dancing bears and talking frogs.

Of course the well-crafted messages we receive say that if we eat more of this, drink more of that, have this in our wardrobe or this parked on a dock or in a garage, we will be happier. And we spend *billions* in search of happiness. The problem is that the object of our gluttony does not bring us happiness. We don't enjoy the object of our gluttony. We merely consume it. And then we are bloated with what we have consumed but not one inch closer to happiness than we were when we started out.

Americans are making and spending more than ever before, but it doesn't seem to be getting them anywhere. There are more antidepressants on the market. Apparently consumption and the quest for happiness are not nearly as related as we might imagine. Happiness has something more to do with an inner disposition. Happy people have answered some important questions. Who am I? Why am I here? Where am I going? Happy people have relationships that are ends, rather than means to an end. They don't consume relationships to get what they want. They thrive on relationships because relationships with God and others are what life is all about. Happy people use what they have very well. They spend very little time worrying about what they don't have.

Just over twenty years ago, 35 percent of all Americans said that they were very happy. Two decades and a staggering dose of prosperity later, only 29 percent say they are very happy, while the number of very unhappy people has risen dramatically.

Of all the Seven Deadly Sins, gluttony is perhaps the one sin where we see some encouragement and improvement in our society at large.

Concerns about ecology and scarcity are making us more conscious of the choices we make. Recycling, energy consciousness, concern about food waste and physical health are all very positive signs that we are beginning to wrestle with our consumerism. Perhaps we humans are heading into a time of unprecedented spiritual enlightenment in which we are recognizing things as idols—as false gods—and jettisoning them, or at least putting them in service in the proper perspective.

A sociologist observed a significant movement in our culture asserting that voluntary simplicity is living in a way that is outwardly simpler and inwardly richer. There are over three dozen newsletters available in the marketplace on downshifting and simplicity. People seem to be longing for something more in which the more does not mean more to consume. Ten thousand baby boomers turn fifty every day and about 5 percent (one out of twenty) boomers report intentional downshifting.

Downshifting is the act of simplifying life. Less frenzy. Less work. Less striving. Working with what one has, and enjoying it fully. We know that gluttony is a problem for us. I see so many adults cashing out at midlife. They refuse to be a rat in the rat race. Instead they are restoring dignity and meaning to their humanity. What I observe in the high-tech cash-outs and the intentional downshifting that is going on is a deep desire to return to sanity. One insightful writer, Bob Buford, says that enlightened spiritual people tend to make a transition at midlife, moving from success to significance.

A survey funded by a family foundation to learn more about consumption and materialism discovered that 90 percent of Americans feel that the "buy now, pay later" attitude causes us to consume more than we need. Twenty-eight percent of those surveyed said that they had made intentional moves away from gluttonous consumerism.

Gluttony causes us to buy it all now and pay later with our very souls. And do we ever pay. Why do I do this? It sounds so off base, so ill-advised. My answer: Gluttony has such a hold on me that I just take the bait. In some ways, I abdicate my will to choose by giving myself over to gluttony. I like the thrill of the hunt for more things and more experiences. I like the fresh taste of something new and more. Besides, I am so busy holding on to the earth, that I simply do not think.

Working against the effects of gluttony begins with the act of letting go of the earth and attaching ourselves to things eternal. This is what it means to be holy.

Christians have been sold a load of garbage concerning the meaning of the word "holiness." We have been told it means to be morally and spiritually perfect. For some the definition of holiness is walking quietly through life, skirting this world. Far from it! The word "holy," which comes from the Greek word *hagios*, means "to be set apart for a purpose." Understanding ourselves as unique miracles from God, each with a destiny and life mission, locks us into a more constructive view of the world and ourselves. Now the world is not something to cling to, but rather something to engage, nurture, and even change. I bet you'd like to be this kind of holy, wouldn't you?

As we align our worldview with that of heaven, instead of the earth, we can become more aware of the demands made upon us by a clinging, consuming, wasteful culture. We find ourselves actually longing to hang on to heaven. I think we are getting tired of what we see as we look at ourselves and at our culture. I am willing to admit that the consumerism and wastefulness are getting to me. And, I am not alone in the desire for change.

I recently took a Christian magazine publisher to lunch to discuss a project. We walked into a Chinese food buffet. It was well stocked, and we both cautioned each other against excess going in. We avoided a gluttonous binge.

But the real shocker was discovering no less than five signs inside the restaurant that said, "Welcome. Please eat all you would like. But don't take more than you eat. Please help us avoid waste."

I visited quickly with the manager who said they weren't posting the signs just to increase profits. They were posting the signs because they have moved here from a country where wastefulness was an abhorrent behavior. He told me that while he is learning much about America, maybe we could learn something from him.

I think that restaurant manager is embarking on a noble endeavor. Gluttony is very much tied to wastefulness. The consumed object that is "more than enough" is wasted, but so are the time, effort, and energy of interacting with that object. Gluttony sucks more life out of us than we might wish to imagine. This is no more true in any area than that of weight loss. While technically weight loss occurs when we burn off more than we take in, some diet plans are now focusing less on counting calories consumed and calories expended and instead on eating when one is hungry, and no more. That means we have to learn what hunger feels like, to listen to our bodies and our minds.

Most of us commit sins of gluttony because we never do feel what it's really like to be hungry—to need something. The follow-up to this sort of consume-only-when-truly-hungry strategy is to stop consuming once you have had enough.

The need for change in our lives and in our society has many manifestations. I am not one to enjoy going on a negative tirade and condemning things. I don't want anyone to feel condemned by a story or an attribute of a sin to which they can relate very strongly. This book is not about pointing out your sin or my sin and condemning. It's about honest self-reflection and enlightenment with an eye toward growth.

I think intentionally countering sins like gluttony is more exciting than just stopping bad habits; it's a matter of developing good habits that nourish the soul. This is what I love about the life and teachings of Jesus Christ. He once noted that His yoke was easy and His burden was light. He welcomed weary pilgrims to a positive and better way. Jesus Christ, God in human costume, is the compelling leader of a new way, the New Creation. Jesus is our guide, and our guide is all about love. Each one of us has the ability to be a great lover, because we are so very loved by God.

Love is what it is all about. Each of the Seven Deadly Sins blocks out, inhibits, or distorts love. I remember a song, popular with the Jesus People in the early 1970s, that included the line, "Jesus reduce me to love." The cry of the song, beginning to end, is to experience and circulate the outrageous love of God. As we carry the burdens of our cumulative flaws and the grief they bring our way, as we chafe and blister under the bondage of habits that once brought pleasure but now own us, it's a relief to know that God has some good news. That news is that God is deeply in love with us and profoundly committed to our welfare and progress.

Alongside God's good news of redeeming love, there is often the bad news—sins like gluttony corrupt and defile love and all that is lovely. Our internal eye for God becomes clouded and dull. Our receptivity to pure love from God is sublimated to the love of pure consumption. Concentration on consumption isolates the consumer. Gluttony misses life and love by elevating a piece of life to an astronomically exaggerated level. A piece of life becomes the whole of life. We find ourselves in a place where compulsions scream for us to do this, do that, buy this, buy that. We go nearly insane with the volume and persistence of these compulsive inner voices and we miss the quiet voice of God.

This is the nature of addiction. Addiction begins when a substance of some sort (food, sex, drugs, adventure, clothing) becomes lord and master of a human soul. The substance is no longer something used by the consumer. It consumes and controls the consumer. We, the addicted, wind up used, wasted, and discarded by the very thing that has charmed us.

One of the things that is tough about gluttony is that it often deals with objects with which we must interact to survive. We need clothing. We need to look after our health. We need to eat and drink. It can be very difficult to consume what we need, while holding these things at arm's length lest they come to own us.

Not all gluttony is attributable to addiction. But all addiction stems from gluttony. Just because you and I may not be food addicts, drug addicts, or the like doesn't mean we are free from gluttony. What it probably means is that we are not advanced to the point of addiction and obsession. Or, perhaps we have some form of inner governor that keeps us on the safe side of addiction. Just because we are not clinically addicted to something doesn't mean that it can't hurt us.

A couple of examples will help here. The first is a confession on my part. I am a Type-A person who thrives on stress and activity. My adrenal glands are always pumping. I come very close to being addicted to the high. Every couple of years I have personal meltdowns that cause me to rethink my pace and confess my gluttonous consumption of adrenaline and my gluttonous tendency to consume experiences. I tell myself the lie that I can and will do it all. It's a really poor attempt at control.

One doesn't have to be an alcoholic to have an alcohol issue. My second example of nonaddictive gluttonous behavior is the story of a friend of mine, who reported that he had proven he was not an alcoholic through proper assessment. I accepted that he wasn't an alcoholic. A number of months later this person was inebriated while on the way to a resort. He drove his car off the road in a spectacular crash and was lucky to live. It was also fortunate that he didn't kill anyone else. He may not have been clinically classified as an alcoholic, but his propensity for heavy drinking sure enough caused him serious grief. Addiction, no. Gluttony, yes.

I mentioned the overall gravity afforded consumerism in our culture. This tendency to consume is energetically supported in communities. There is much fellowship in the sin of gluttony. For instance, drinkers hang out together because the pot's not going to call the kettle black.

I consider it a privilege to marry young couples who are serious about their faith and about their life together. I want those wedding ceremonies to be beautiful, dignified, and fun. I recently had a disaster, which left me incensed and very near the point of canceling a wedding. The groom, a recovering alcoholic, invited two of his former drinking buddies to be in the wedding, so as to honor their longtime friendship. The groom was proud of his recovery and deeply transformed by his newfound faith in Jesus Christ as Lord and Savior. He had not touched alcohol for a number of years. What spoiled this great event was the behavior of the two groomsmen.

These two men spent the entire day drunk. They showed up drunk at the church for the pictures before the wedding, then sneaked down the street and continued drinking at a bar, boasting later, "That place is a lush's bar. It's got the stiffest drinks in the city!" Both of these pathetic groomsmen made fools of themselves before, during, and after the wedding.

I felt so sorry for the young couple who had trusted them. In addition to ruining a holy event, these two showed enormous disrespect for both their friend and his bride.

This ugly encounter with the fellowship of drunks reminds me to say something else about gluttony. Gluttony is carelessness of beauty. There is no beauty in the way that a dog eats. You lay a dog's food out in any sort of lovely presentation and your efforts will go ignored. The dog will automatically go face down in the bowl and gulp the food with nary a breath. That's what gluttony looks like. It's gross and ugly in all of its forms. It vandalizes what is beautiful and good.

When you see someone live in moderation and exercise self-control, or as Aristotle would say, practice sobriety, you see the beauty in that person's life. And those of us who manage to develop the inner and outer virtue of self-control see the world more clearly. Without the inebriation of "things" to which we cling, we see more beauty in more places and in more people. This is life as it is meant to be.

In the end, gluttony seems to me to be a misuse of God-given gifts. Gluttony in all its forms places our trust in things we consume rather than God. There is a God-shaped vacuum in the heart of every human being which only God can satisfy. But in our brokenness and self-determined effort to do things our way, we will try to put just about anything in the God-void, except God. God is too real, too absolute for many of us. God is so absolute that we run from Him in fear thinking that we can dodge His presence. And as we scramble in our restless flight from absolute reality, we attach ourselves to objects that are unreal in the sense that they cannot be gods. We make gods of things like food, electronic toys, automobiles, and many other items. We try all too hard to fill the God-shaped vacuum in our lives with something other than God. Most of us become aware at some point that these objects are not God, that they don't fulfill. Yet, we also find ourselves trapped in our own history of habitual misuse.

To the degree that gluttony is misplaced faith, the sin of gluttony is abandonment of self-control. Self-control is accessed when we long—heart, body, mind, and soul—to know God, to put things in their right place, and use God-given gifts to generate faith, hope, and love in our world. Items of consumption move from an addictive motivational role, to a more sustaining role. They become tools to live a meaningful life. God is the subject and object of life, not an obsession with a mere thing.

So, one spiritual prophylaxis for gluttony is self-control. Self-control is the act of integrating what we know into who we are and what we do. Self-control emerges as we grow in understanding who God has created us to be—and then living out our role in this world. Self-control means managing our energies and desires. The purity self-control brings to us is that we become focused upon whom we are becoming and how we offer ourselves to this world.

A friend of mine recently told me about an eye-opening experience he had while playing in a college football game. Frustrated by himself and his team as they fell way behind their opponent, this young football player laid a dirty hit on a member of the other team at the sideline of the field. The opposing coach shouted, "Come on number fifty-five, you're better than that."

Self-control would have helped my friend. He is indeed better than that which he displayed on a difficult afternoon of football. In the same manner, we are better than what we settle for in gluttony. We are created by God for a purpose. We have a destiny. We are each a unique and unrepeatable miracle. Self-control puts us beyond the reach of instinctual, instantaneous urges and helps us remember who we really are.

The wonderful thing about self-control is that it is forged over a lifetime. I see too many spiritual pilgrims convert to being followers of Jesus Christ and then expect to see their behavior totally changed in the first year. It doesn't work that way. Any good spiritual progress in your life and mine comes with time, a dash of suffering, and a commitment to steady improvement.

A dear man named John Garlington was a superb pastor in Buffalo, New York, and then Portland, Oregon. He was full of wisdom and much wit. He came from an African-American family of ministers. John was a loving, entertaining, and very vulnerable man. He knew how to tell the truth without hurting others.

When I was a young minister, John Garlington became a bit of a mentor to me. I used to share all kinds of plans to help people mature spiritually. He would listen so kindly. He would nod. Then, during one of my pontifications, John said, "Randy, just remember, we're growin' trees, not cabbages."

We cannot expect to live kitchen garden lives, where the bounty blossoms into the fullest proportion in just one season. Instead, we grow like trees: one ring per year. Steadily. Surely. Taller. Wider. Deeper. Denser. The growth is hardly perceptible unless measured by decades. But the rewards are outstanding.

It's the same with the effects of self-control in our lives. Self-control begins and sustains a process of growth and change. It is very "core" business that self-control does. It goes right to our essence as human beings. Who am I? Why am I here? Where am I going? Why do I do what I do? For whom do I do what I do? What first attracted me to conspicuous consumption?

Self-control seeks the answers to these questions, directs us to faith in God during our Herculean struggles with the forces that have corrupted us. Self-control gives us the courage to be intentional and make a stand. And tiny victories in self-control imbue us with the courage to keep going forward, even when the gains are small.

The Apostle Paul and Aristotle both place this virtue on their list. To be self-controlled means to have the inner spiritual resources to triumph over destructive inner voices that want to rule us. This is the ultimate act of taking responsibility for our lives.

Self-control sounds like some act of extreme stoicism practiced by flat, emotionless, nonpassionate people. And, to be honest, examples of this kind of stoicism mark the Christian church and alienate many of us from the idea of self-control. But self-control is more than a rigid resolve to do this or not do that. It is, more significantly, a deep inner knowledge of self. Self-control leads us to beware of where we might slip up and hurt ourselves or others. Self-control is in touch with our desire for an inner climate of peace, joy, and harmony. Self-control asserts itself against the voice of gluttony in order to protect what is precious inside each of us.

One of the problems most of us have with self-control is that our sin abrogates against self-control's process. We want instant gratification. We want answers and results now. Why in the world would anyone want to work for a decade to exhibit a modicum of self-control over wrong eating habits that translate as gluttony? Not me. I am fond of the signs on the roadside that say, "LOSE 30 POUNDS IN 30 DAYS." These signs are as false as bathroom graffiti that says, "For a good time, call Joan at 555-9099." But until you and I accept the patience God lavishes on us and practice a little patience with ourselves, we will not make progress against the deadly sin of gluttony. As I wrote earlier, waiting out the urges to see if hunger is real or imagined takes patience.

Do you even remember the days before answering machines and voice mail? We all had to jump and answer the phone. The phone was a huge distraction for most professionals. There was no "Do not disturb" button on the phone set as I have in my office. The hardest thing in the world was to keep working or just hold still long enough for the phone to stop ringing. Our urge to be in touch, to answer on one ring, is very similar to our bent toward conspicuous consumption. The urges hit hard. We reflexively reach to answer the phone or eat something. Patience. Waiting. Just a few seconds of patience and waiting and some very strong urges pass us by.

A noted expert in alcohol abuse treatment commented in a recent publication that alcoholics who come to God and admit their powerlessness begin, over time, to discover an inner power given them by God, the ultimate higher power. What this man went on to describe is a process wherein the person who could once only say "yes" to alcohol now could indeed say "yes" and "no" and simply chooses to say "no."

I believe what is happening with the people I have just described is that they have received from God the gift of self-control. This gift might start small, but it produces great results over a lifetime. It doesn't happen overnight. It doesn't happen without patience and courage. But, it does happen. We begin becoming whole.

When we are dealing with our addictions, appetites, and drives, we are touching on the hardest and most painful of all issues to address in human life. We are tearing at the very fabric of the false illusions that make so many of our lives tolerable on a day-to-day basis, yet disastrous in the long run.

And if you and I think gluttony is a tough topic to cover, then we had better really brace ourselves for the subject of lust. Next in the sins we love.

NINE

It's Okay to Look ... Isn't It?: LUST

In the 1970s and 1980s, I worked as a disc jockey on a popular rock radio station in the Seattle area. When you are a disc jockey you work frantically during your entire show to stay on top of things—contests, traffic problems, weather, special features, etc. There is little time for anything else, with few exceptions. But one of the exceptions is that a disc jockey gets to listen to lots of music, played nice and loud. I must have the lyrics and melodies of thousands of songs memorized.

One very popular song on the country western charts crossed over to the Top 40 format in which I worked. The song's sad chorus was, "Looking for love in all the wrong places, looking for love in all the wrong faces."

That song has haunted me through the years. It is the story of most of us human beings. We live in a world in which people are dying to be loved and don't know where on earth to find love and intimacy. We all desire to know and be known, to love and be loved. But intimacy escapes us as we look for love in all the wrong places. Intimacy escapes us when we confuse sexual fascination and desire with love.

Not a single one of us doesn't desire intimacy. And true intimacy is powerful. Phillip Sheldrake in *Befriending Our Desires* says:

> *Only within our experiences of intimacy with other people, whether genital or not, may we learn a way of being fully personally present both to ourselves and to others rather than being superficial and remote in our emotional lives. The risk of intimacy rather than the apparent security of emotional detachment reveals the truth of our selves, teaches us about availability and educates us in truthful self disclosure. Of all human experiences intimacy is the one most likely to provoke real change in us.*

There are many hungers and longings that churn within the hearts of human beings. But no hunger is perhaps greater or more powerful than the drive for intimacy when it is united with the sex drive. Many will try to argue that this is a male problem. After years of pastoral counseling, I no longer support this notion. Seeking sexual excitement, deeper intimacy, sensual pleasure, and daydreaming about things erotic are an issue for all humans.

Lust is an overdeveloped love of the sensual and erotic. It is a distortion of the love shared between those who share intimacy. Rather than being focused on another, the love is absorbed in titillation, pleasure, fantasy.

I am sure that all of us have had the experience of losing control of our faculties and making poor sexual decisions. Some of those decisions have included irresponsible or immoral sexual expressions. Others experience the entire distortion of lust in the theater of the mind. Whether we experience our sexual distortions as real physical acts or as fantasies, both are a part of the sin called lust.

Lust is a fixation with the thought of sex. And, according to the folks in the field of medicine and psychology, we think a lot about sex. Where is the line between thinking and dwelling? It's hard to tell. But it occurs to me that normative behavior stops and the sin of lust has its onset at the point you or I dwell upon a sexually attractive person and begin building scenarios which emerge as fantasy. This dwelling upon the sexual trigger can emerge as images of sexual encounters. There are numerous magazines and the entire Internet to feed this displaced sexual urge and take it to great heights. For some, the lust may be more subtle. In this case the day-dreaming or fantasy is one of the perfect life in the perfect home. This sort of fantasy may give great pleasure by distracting us from who we are and what we have. Romance novels are famous for creating this sort of lust.

In the New Testament, the Apostle Paul uses the word *porneia* to describe a sexual sin associated with lust. It gets right at the idea of dwelling that I have been discussing. *Porneia* means to artificially stimulate and feed the sexual triggers within us. You know by now the word Paul is using is our word pornography. Normal attraction ends at the point where we feed the original thought to artificially stimulate a sexual response. You see, God knows that most of us have a sexual drive that is plenty strong. It does not need to be fed.

Recent research does confirm that almost all of us view persons of the opposite sex asking ourselves with at least subtle curiosity, "What would it be like to have a sexual experience with this person?" If this is so, we must attack lust at the first wink of the eye or turn of the head when we encounter those whom we might find sexually attractive.

A researcher on male sexuality has recorded that men think of sex up to sixty times per hour. Women tend to think of sex at least a few times an hour. We cannot avoid thoughts of sex. We cannot avoid recognizing that the people around us are sexual beings. To think we can is a dangerous fantasy. We must recognize our sexual nature. But how do we acknowledge that we are sexual beings, acknowledge our sexual impulses and feelings, and yet not wind up becoming fixated on them? Can we be sexual beings and not be lust-mongers?

"Lust" comes from the Latin word *luxuria*, which means to overindulge for the purpose of pleasure. Lust can refer to a lust for money, power, success, or fame. But while there are various forms of lust, the sexual form is the most common and most pronounced. Because the sexual expression of lust is such a huge issue in our sex-crazed society, we will focus on the sexual aspects of lust. If this is not your issue, consider yourself fortunate, and read the rest of this chapter substituting power or fame or whatever you might lust after.

When our built-in attraction to someone results in a fixation on sexual considerations, lust is the name of the game. When we luxuriate in the idea of what it would be like to engage in sexual contact with another person, we enter into the domain of lust. Lust is a sin we love because it can make us feel good. It deceives us into thinking that we are passionate. Lust hangs out a sign before us that reads, "THIS IS WHAT YOU HAVE ALWAYS WANTED. THIS WILL MAKE YOUR LIFE COMPLETE."

I remember when I was an undergraduate there was an administrator on campus who sponsored the "Lust Club." Members developed lists of the most lusty ladies in the world and then added a customized list of women on campus who were truly "lust-worthy." Meetings of the lust club were often held in a common area on campus where members could ogle coeds and declare some "lust-worthy." I found this celebration of lust quite odd. It was uncomfortable for me. Sure, I was guilty of having done privately what this group did publicly, but I could not bring myself to celebrate an issue which I reckoned to be sin within me.

To declare someone lust-worthy is to reduce them to a sexual creature. That's dehumanizing. Lust dehumanizes by devaluing or minimizing another human. Lust also degrades us. It's one of those things that lurks in the heart of us like a can of gas—and there always seem to be so many burning matches around. Lust burns. It causes an internal conflagration. A firestorm.

If you are anything like me, you know what lust feels like. You know how it sneaks up on you and how tricky it becomes. And most of us are a little ashamed about lust. We don't like to talk about it with our best of friends, our spouses, or anyone else. It's embarrassing to feel so out of control and not be able to explain why. Lust is so overpowering at its onset that many of us lose our sense of rational thought and reflection.

Let me take a risk by sharing for a moment. I am a happily married man. I am also a red-blooded male. Not so long ago, after officiating at a wedding ceremony, a stunning, tall, dark-haired woman with a figure that would make Stevie Wonder turn his head came over to the table where I was sitting and began flirting with me. During our conversation, she told me that she liked my voice and that she hoped to find a guy her age that reminded her of me.

I was on fire. I did everything I could to shake the encroaching lust, but the flames were out of control. In an attempt to find some objectivity, I even told this woman that I would be happy to make myself available to preside at her wedding ceremony when she found the right guy. Even this noble attempt to be honorable didn't work. I was still filled with lust.

Finally, I panicked. I said I had to leave to return home to my wife and kids who were expecting me. I rushed out of the reception room and got to my car where I was literally pouring sweat. As I exited the parking garage I audibly thanked God for saving me from myself by giving me the courage and self-control to leave the scene of my potential crimes. On the way home, I asked God for more of whatever it takes inside me to do battle with lust.

I have taken a risk here in sharing about my own journey. In 1976, when Jimmy Carter admitted that he had "looked on a lot of women with lust," it nearly cost him the election as President of the United States. Carter's admission hit too close to home for many of us. We aren't perfect, but we want our heroes to be. I don't want people admitting their lust to me, lest I universalize lust as normative and become even more motivated in practicing lust. Plus, most of us are ashamed of our lust. We rationalize that we just weren't being ourselves when it last took hold of us. The hideousness of lust is that we internalize it and through a shame base (which I discussed earlier in this book) we actually build more and more triggers for lust and make even more room for it in our lives.

Another thing about lust is that few of us will talk about it. Expressing what we are thinking and feeling would make us seem like a beast. So, we smolder quietly, trying to hide the beast of lust within. But most of us have found the hard way that lust cannot be contained, for the smoldering fire burns hot. We cannot just ignore lust and figure that it will go away.

Our Creator knows how our bodies work. God gave you and me our sex drives. (It's part of what he called "very good.") God recognizes that we have powerful sexual urges. In one New Testament letter, the Apostle Paul advises, "It is better to marry than to burn." Nancy and I liked this verse so much that we had it printed on matchbooks and we handed them out in the reception line at our wedding.

God has hardwired us with sexual function, a hair-trigger sex drive, and focused reaction to sexual stimulation. This is wonderful with a lifetime partner. It can be frightening around anyone else.

A young couple I know has formed a very successful musical duo that travels quite a bit. They live a fast-paced, hardworking life. Their alternative rock music is excellent. They even get some radio airplay. One of their songs, entitled "Brains Head South," is about lust. The hook in the chorus is "let's stop and cool off before our brains head south."

For those of us who have been victimized by lust, we know just how true this duo's lyrics ring. There are all kinds of jokes about people thinking with their gonads. It's not a joke. A good onslaught of lust makes the sufferer feel like all the blood in her body has flowed to sexual regions and that her brain has relocated in sexual climes where pure unbridled passion and desire drive the brain's very function.

One of the reasons we really don't want our brains to head south is our personal desire for integration. We realize in our moments of reflection that our persons are made of a mix of tangible and non-tangible elements. We are part soul and spirit. We are part intellect. We are also physical. Integrity or personal integration is harmonizing what we believe, think, say, and do. This integration is very hard between the soul and emotional centers and the physical body that is exposed to this world of pleasure and pain. The body doesn't enjoy the buffers it offers to the inner person. The body is the surface or shell. But our bodies do matter.

Flesh is integrally connected to all the other parts that make up our unique persons. We cannot be free to be fully human until we are able to manage our physical bodies with some degree of success.

A woman suffering from a long series of failed romances with men who had used her, cheated on her, stolen from her, and humiliated her sat in my office recounting her woes. She expressed that about the only thing that worked with all of the men who had hurt her was sex. I asked why she was having sex with people who didn't express any more respect for her than they had. This young woman suddenly became indignant. She bitterly said, "I don't see why sex is such a big deal. If that's something I want and a guy wants it, I give it. Why wait until later in the relationship?"

I wanted to answer, "Wait! See if there is a commitment to you before giving your body to that person," but I bit my tongue instead and a few minutes later she went her way. I sat in my office, sad for this young woman. I knew that her sexuality and the indulging in lust had become convoluted and that she was going to have a tough time for the foreseeable future.

You see, sexuality is a big deal. If God is Creator, our ability to procreate by way of sex could in fact be one of the strongest ways in which you and I bear the image of God. Asking someone to participate in a creative act like sex is a little different than inviting someone out for ice cream. Sex is not something we just do. It is creative and life changing, even life forming.

Sexuality is a way we express ourselves intimately in the midst of a time and space world. It is our enterprise of creativity and unconditional love.

I have mentioned earlier in this book that the word "holy" means to be set apart for a purpose. As followers of Christ, we are becoming the kind of people who are learning to love. Love, which Aristotle defines as "seeking the highest good for another" cannot express itself in or around a context of lust. Aristotle's definition of love is further amplified by the Greek of the New Testament where the word *agape* is introduced. *Agape* means complete and unconditional love, even sacrificial love. Built into the very fabric of love is attentiveness to the other. Love is not love unless it is lost in the other. Lust is self-reflective love. It makes an object of others.

Lust firebombs real love. The way we love matters, though. We are designed to live our lives in ways that seek the best for others, in ways that show respect for others. We are also built to negotiate our relationships honestly. One of the things about lust is that it motivates us to potentially make implied promises or commitments that we cannot keep. When lust is burning, whether for sex, power, or even fame, promises are easily made and good intentions are expressed. The problem is that the good intentions and promises are reckoned null and void once *luxuria* has fed itself. Lust misdirects us. The object of our urges is just that: an object. When we are through receiving from the object, we dispose of it. All promises and agreements are terminated.

I don't know how many times I have counseled young people in my office who were victims of lust. The majority were young women. They dated a man. The relationship was sexual from the beginning. She lived with the superficiality and the sex thinking that intimacy with the guy would be forthcoming. But then when she asked what he was thinking, and particularly what he was thinking about the relationship between the two of them, he first emotionally and then physically disappeared.

Intimacy, by definition, is a covenantal promise to understand the depths of another and stand with them for the long haul. But many of us, afflicted by the fire of lust, wind up deceiving others in order to feed our lust.

Lust seems so strong that most of us would figure that it is an overfunctioning of the God-given sex drive. But I have come to think of it as the opposite. Lust is the underfunctioning of love and sexuality as God intended it to be. I opened this chapter with a quote from an expert in spirituality and sexuality. His comments about intimacy describe what most of us deeply desire. When fear, poor self-esteem, and other internal forces repel us from our true desire, lust is what we wind up settling for.

We fear rejection, abandonment, alienation, failure to be lovable and adequate in relationships. These insecurities drive us to what we feel are safer places to explore our sensual and erotic urges. In doing so, we underfunction. We become less than what God created us for. You see, love and sexuality are meshed together in the context of a committed relationship. Herein the fire is productive. Sexual intimacy is a bonding agent.

Sexual fixation and sexual episodes outside of monogamous lifelong commitments do not foster an environment of genuine love. Any feelings of love are more likely the self-love of personal gratification more than they are a result of seeking the highest good for another. Lust, when acted upon, leaves its objects heartbroken, confused, and used. I find it hard to think that someone would sincerely say, "I had that one-night stand so that I could make him/her a happier, healthier, better person."

On the contrary victims of our lust often feel terrible. To protect themselves and justify past acts these persons allow the inner places of their heart to become scarred and callous.

I recall one particularly sad encounter with a woman who was deeply damaged by lust. She was an attractive college student with a bright mind, and a mature model's body. She was deeply spiritual and very committed to her faith. She was definitely a person I would have expected to do very well in life.

She came to visit me in obvious pain. As she entered my office, she looked as if she carried the world on her shoulders. She went on to admit that she had gotten sexually involved with a couple of guys. The men knew each other well and each was familiar with the other's exploits of her, often comparing notes, and even worse, telling her. However, she wasn't taking notes on these men's sexual skills; she was hoping for genuine love.

She went on to tell me that she had always been a very sensual person. She loved being cuddled and hugged by her parents. She loved back rubs and foot rubs. She loved to snuggle with her sisters in front of the television set.

In a moment of anguish, this dear woman shared her deepest thoughts with me. I was honored, but I hurt for her. She said, "I just need to be held. I wanted to find a guy who I liked who would just hold me—you know, just let me sit in their lap and hold me. I gave into the sexual stuff convincing myself that if I gave them what they wanted, perhaps they would give me what I wanted." She reluctantly gave of herself in a way she knew might cause herself damage, all for the possibility of being held. The men she had been with were obvious victims of lust, but she was, too. She tried to get what she felt she really needed, but in an inappropriate way.

I really respect this woman. I feel her pain. Her story is a glaring example of what happens when our brains head south. Rather than seeking the highest good for another, lust when acted upon devalues its object. Worse yet, I am convinced that the one lusting is also devalued. The positive possibilities of love are absent.

A middle-aged woman, married and with two lovely children, visited me some time ago. She had a real problem. She had met a man during a visit to one of her company's clients and found him to be some sort of projection of "the man of her dreams." By the time this woman returned from the client's office, she was already building a mental image of a life together with this mystery man. She hardly knew him, yet he had captured all of her emotional energy and her desires for intimacy.

The woman realized that her fantasies were distracting her from what was real and important to her. She also had come to a point where she was having a hard time turning off her wandering thoughts. She was trapped in active lust and the cost to her was great. Her self-esteem was dropping. Her confidence that she was a godly woman, a follower of Christ, was diminished. She perceived that she was devaluing herself by lusting, but didn't know how to escape. After taking the first step of acknowledging her lust as sin, she's doing better, with God's grace and the help of some expert Christian counseling.

Devaluation of the self happens when psychological damage leaves someone unable to function normally. Larry was a respectable man from the East Coast. Which is why he drove up to eighty miles from home to vent his lust at peep shows and triple-X-rated movie houses. He was hooked. And he was so hooked that he was beginning to have trouble accounting for his lost time. He had pornographic magazines and videos hidden around his home and office.

At the same time, he was finding the pornography less and less stimulating, so he increased his dose and sought more hard-core materials. Eventually, he was left with no ability to become sexually stimulated in intimate situations with his wife. And finally the pornography was no longer giving him a rush. Pornography refused to be his servant any longer, and tragically, he became lust's slave. That's one characteristic each of the Seven Deadly Sins share in common. In fact, they wouldn't be the sins we love if we really came to grips with the reality of things. Lust and the other deadly sins tempt us to exercise them in search of fulfillment, but they don't fulfill. They degrade, devalue, and destroy us—and others.

My friend's story has a happy ending. Prayer, meditation, worship, counseling, and help from his wife got him well. Yes, I said help from his wife. My friend confessed all to her, hoping she wouldn't leave—and she didn't. He swears that her unconditional love and support of him were decisive. It was the model of true love that could lift him.

My friend has recovered well. He has sexual intimacy at home and sexual continence when it comes to the use of pornographic materials. Not everyone is so lucky.

I have another friend who, like me, grew up in the sixties. Very few of us who lived through the sexual revolution practiced sexual purity. My friend tells some sad stories about what the promiscuity of his early years has done to him.

He said that because of all the sexual variety he had experienced, it was very difficult to focus his sexual energy on his spouse. Further, he said, he had no conscience in regard to sexuality. He said he mostly didn't do anything wrong sexually because he kept himself busy. However, on those occasions when he slipped, he admitted that he had no bad feelings about it. This condition is called a seared conscience. But the encouraging thing about my friend is that while his conscience didn't operate fully, he still had some knowledge of right and wrong and he chose what was right because it was right. His faithfulness was not based on emotion. It was based on doing what was right. We can survive this way, but it's tough. One of the consequences of runaway sin is the seared conscience, where the tenderness and emotional responses that lead to obedience are damaged.

My friend also reported that he experienced very little sexual satisfaction with his wife and that he was virtually unable to relate to the word "intimacy" as an emotional connection between two people. His misuse of his physical sex drive had warped his ability to engage deeply and vulnerably in a relationship. Summarizing his situation, he said, "Free love cost me everything."

Failing to respect others sexually eventually ruins our own self-respect and functionality as sexual beings. The great philosopher, Immanuel Kant, spoke strongly for the intrinsic value of all people. He noted that people are always ends, never a means. To make a person a "means to an end" is to objectify him—to make him an object for a specific use rather than a person of intrinsic worth. In the case of lust, a person becomes a means of sexual stimulation, whether that stimulation comes through physical contact or mental fantasy. Rather than valuing others, we reduce them to offerings in the fires of our lust.

On the other hand, love treats a person as an end. This is what God hopes for all of our interactions. This is the positive side of Kant's dictum. People are always ends. To treat another as an end is to grant her individuality and worth simply for who she is. Kant, a deeply Christian man, had to be thinking of the words of Jesus and the actions of Jesus. Jesus treated all persons as humans. He imparted value to people, he didn't drain value from them for his own purposes. "Greater love has no man than that he lay down his life for another" is the supreme expression of other-love. Jesus met the broken and gave them something that made them whole. Jesus made people subject, ends, never means to a selfish end.

If we truly desire to view and relate to others as subjects, how do we move beyond the almost primal power of lust?

If lust is a fire, how is it to be contained? I think two of Paul's virtues become powerful tools in the battle to control lusty impulses. The first is patience and the second, similar to its use in the battle with gluttony, is self-control.

Patience? Where does patience come into things? Well, simply this: If we can still ourselves and wait, good sense prevails and good things happen. Patience believes that God has the best in mind for us and is willing to wait for our Creator to provide fulfillment of our hopes, dreams, needs, longings, and desires.

When a young couple is dating and both are burning to express their growing love toward one another, every molecule in their bodies says, "Let's do it." When a single man lives alone, his biweekly trip to the video store parades him past shelves full of adult movies and (maybe after a look over his shoulder to see if friends or neighbors are in the store) every molecule inside of him screams, "Just do it." When a married person feels unfulfilled emotionally and sexually by a partner and sees a potential new sexual partner every molecule inside him screams, "You deserve more than you are getting. Make a move!" A single woman has fantasies of intimacy and a desire to share her body physically and so she says "yes" to an invitation home to a man's house after a first date.

When our bodies are screaming, as all of them do at times, we believe that if we do not act upon the lust we are feeling, we will be consumed by it. We feel it will get worse and worse until we become some frothing monster or that we might explode into flames.

But the fact is that all of the physiological and psychological triggers that come into play in sexual arousal have a rise, a peak, and a denouement. It is proven that if one has the patience to wait a sexually stimulating situation out for a few minutes, control can be regained. Patience tells us that we don't need to let our brains head south.

Self-control works alongside patience. As we practice patience and see the cycles of interest and arousal run their course without acting out sexually, we develop a sense of mastery. The Greek word for self-control that Paul uses in the fruit of the Spirit is *egratia*, which means "mastery."

Self-control is forged out of deep self-knowledge, lots of experience, the pain and agony of failures, and determined practice.

We have observed that for each of the sins we love, there is a distortion of true love for which true love becomes curative. It's the same with lust. God has built us to be sexual beings, to have urges and desires. These longings are part of what it means to be human. Lust so imitates the real desires God creates in us that making progress against lust takes a process of a divinely shaped evolution of the Spirit, mind, and will to be able to deal with primal issues. But would you and I rather be able to say that we are determined and controlled by more than just the brain stem? I for one would like to leave this world numbered among those that accessed more, rather than less, of my gray matter.

Practicing patience and self-control takes knowledge of our own drives. What spins your propeller sexually? What things and what types of persons turn you on? When do your drives peak? What circumstances in life bring overwhelming sexual content into your thought life? Stress? Anger? Fatigue? Feelings of inadequacy? When are you most prone to lust?

While we counter lust by asking and attempting to answer these questions in search of self-control, there are other disciplines that help us push lust away from the center of our lives. They're called fellowship and accountability. I see fellowship and accountability as aspects of self-control. In the arena of committed spiritual friendships we openly and vulnerably share our stories knowing that we are loved and accepted. Then, we hold ourselves accountable to these people who love us. For instance, I hold myself accountable to my doctor in treating my health. I have to tell him what is going on with me, listen to his responses, and do what he says if I am to get well.

I am convinced that we all need a small group of people with whom we can be outrageously honest. A place where we can be vulnerable and share all of what's up in us without fear of judgment, yet with an expectation of mutual accountability. We cannot make it alone. We need spiritual companions who will share our struggle.

A friend whom I treasure once called me from a hotel on the East Coast. While appearing as the speaker at a Christian retreat, he ran afoul of a dangerous situation. He met a woman whom he had found very attractive at the retreat. They struck up an ordinary conversation. The chat became more and more flirtatious until the two embraced.

My friend, a married man, invited the woman up to his hotel

room. She accepted, saying she would call shortly, then join him. Forced to practice patience by going to his room and waiting for the tryst to happen, his desire began to drop and his dismay with his situation began to rise. That's when he called me to talk. He said he wanted to keep the phone line blocked so he couldn't take her call and he said, "Just stay on the line with me until this goes away."

About a half hour later, a knock came on the door. It was the woman, looking him up. He, of course, had given her his room number when he had asked her up. While I listened to him, he crossed the room to the door and offered, "I'm sorry, but I'm on an important phone call and it's going to take a while." She left, saying that if he still wanted to get together, he could call her room. He acknowledged her offer, closed the door, bolted it, and came back to the phone. In a few more minutes he felt strong enough to make it and we said good night.

Another colleague of mine took the exact opposite approach. He thought lust was cute. He was a well-known speaker who worked in a ministry to single adults. His denial of lust as an enemy was fatal. His jokes about all of the beautiful single women he was around were continuous.

The talk led to actual behaviors. While speaking at retreats, he gave into lust over and over again, refused to be accountable to anyone, especially to the concerns voiced by his wife. He wounded many already vulnerable people. Finally, he became so brazen (remember our discussion of seared consciences) that he was going to bed with women on the grounds of retreat centers. He was eventually caught in flagrante delicto and his career and marriage were ruined.

Spotting flare-ups early as my wise friend did is so important. We can actually make survival strategies and plans while we are battling lust, before it has taken its full grip on us.

Part of this early warning system is a reminder to hold our center—to keep ourselves fastened to our faith and cognizant of God. We can say things like, "God, I know you gave me this sex drive and it's really hummin' right now. Thanks for the drive and the verification that all the wiring is in place, but will you also help me to control myself here lest I damage you, myself, or another."

God is not a cosmic spoilsport. God wants us to experience joy, intimacy, sensual pleasure, even ecstasy. But he intends for those great moments in life to be bracketed within the context of caring and commitment.

The problem is that when the drumbeat of lust is pounding in our souls, it is very hard to step back and take a long-term perspective. We think, "I need sexual gratification and I need it now. That will take care of the problem." But the gratification doesn't fix things. It fouls them up. There is an old French proverb that contains much wisdom: "You not only have to want what you want, but you also have to want what your want leads to." The big lie that our minds and bodies tell us when lust kicks in is that this seemingly insatiable hunger will not go away unless it's fed. We must have what we want. We must have it now! There is nothing more beyond the all-consuming fire we are experiencing right this moment. Wrong. More likely we are just experiencing a flare-up. It will rise, peak, and decline. But if we give in to the lust we will be living with not only the action of lust, but with all the repercussions that the action set in motion—repercussions that can ripple through many relationships and many years of our lives.

Some patience and self-control will let misplaced desire run its course. Fortunately, patience and self-control, when expressed as fruit of the Spirit, are not the sole product of human striving and exertion of the will. They are fruit borne of an intimate relationship with God. They are fruit expressed as the outworking of the inward divine love we have received from God. This is true for dealing with all sin in our lives, even the sins we love.

Our prayerful, contemplative, and worshipful encounters with God shape our worldview. We get on the same page with God and see things God's way. Our priorities get rearranged and our values shift. Intimacy with God also makes us more aware of ourselves in all of our glory and decadence.

As the Spirit works on our worldview and belief system, we find our attitudes, particularly toward the role of other people in our lives, begin to shift. We sow an attitude and we reap an action. When Scripture tells us "as a person thinks, so they are," we are hearing the wisdom of our Creator. Our attitudes develop thought patterns or thought streams and our thought streams lead to behaviors. Taking positive action from a strong positive motivation is extremely powerful, powerful enough to cause behavioral breakthroughs. The breakthroughs come because actions, when repeated, become habits. And habits, when practiced over the long haul, define, edit, and shape character. Our character finds a natural outlet for itself.

Once again, I think we should spend a lot more time and attention on character development than we do in our society. And we should probably spend a lot less time shaming and heaping guilt on people.

Character development involves listening to stories and learning from them. It involves experimentation. It necessitates failure. It also involves learning from our successes and building a positive track record. It requires courage and endurance, interdependency with others, and the humility to admit where we are. We cannot simply focus on telling ourselves and others what to do. Instead, we must teach ourselves and each other about the sort of people we want to be.

As character takes root, we can initialize attempts to act decisively against the deceitful and overwhelming power of deadly sins, such as lust.

The insatiable desires with which you and I struggle bear a striking similarity to a problem that I had as a little boy. You see, I love dogs. All dogs (well, except poodles, but I even like them). I always had a dog. And I was always desirous of having more dogs.

I walked home from school or sports practice just about every day of the week. I constantly made friends with dogs that would literally follow me home hoping that living under my care would be a better deal for them. More attention, more food.

I think I just about drove my mother insane with continuous pleadings of, "Oh, can't I keep him? She will be easy to care for. I'll feed the dogs."

Mom held her ground with a forceful no. I became more and more fascinated with stray or potentially stray dogs. I got frustrated with Mom's refusal to add another dog to our dog collection, which already had a terrier named Freckles.

In despair, I asked my mom how in the world I was going to cope with this. I mean, after all, the dogs just followed me home and moved in.

Mom's response was a great lesson about animal husbandry, but also an ever-present help in my life with the issue of lust.

"Mom, I can't help it. The dogs are just there. What am I supposed to do, anyway? What do I do with the next dog I find?"

Mom's reply is timeless. "Don't feed it or pet it and it won't follow you home."

Enough said.

TEN

Bring Me a Higher Love: THE PATH OF LOVE

"The only shocking act that remains in the world is love." These words belong to a young actress, but ring with the truth of the ages.

Each of us wants to be a true lover. We desire that our hearts be filled with the love that practices random acts of kindness. We yearn for a life defined by and guided by love. Yet, we live in a world seriously marred by the effects of sin. Each of the Seven Deadly Sins is a category of self-destructive and other-destructive behaviors.

In this book, we have taken a fairly in-depth look at the Seven Deadly Sins: their roots, their outworkings, and their effects. And that leaves us here in this chapter asking, "What do we do about it?"

The first and foremost step is to become fully human by living in intimacy with God. This process of becoming human by a combining of the knowledge of God and the knowledge of self led one church father to say that the glory of God is the human person truly alive. Reformer John Calvin sounds almost twenty-first century in his view that knowledge of self and God, neither to the exclusion of the other, is the seedbed of spiritual progress.

In his opening words to the Institutes of the Christian Religion, Calvin observes, "Our wisdom, in so far as it ought to be deemed true and solid wisdom, consists almost entirely of two parts: the knowledge of God and of ourselves. But these are connected together by many ties, it is not easy to determine which of the two precedes, and gives birth to the other."

Calvin goes on to say that our discovery of self leads to insights about hopes, dreams, and possibilities, but also leads to a deeper understanding of the forces of sin at work in us. A growing knowledge of God reveals God's perfection and like a rheostat on a light, deepening knowledge of God results in a higher intensity light with which we may search our souls for lurking sin. You surely have washed windows on a less than spectacular day. They look pretty good when you are done, but two days later when the sun is out in all of its splendor, your windows show streaks and missed spots. More light, more clarity on the issues and blemishes.

Calvin, Luther, Pope Gregory, modern psychologists, indeed our Risen Lord, Jesus, were all fully aware of the pain involved in this process of continually becoming more and more aware of our sinful nature and our specific sins. For Luther, the corruption of sin was almost treated as a gift. The misery of sin compelled to cry out for a savior. The light of God is bright in our dark spots. But God is not approaching us to condemn us—rather, to make us whole. It is, in fact, the love of God revealed in Jesus Christ that brings us relief: salvation.

In spite of the vision of love in action that we see in Jesus Christ as we read the Gospels, we most often dwell in view of images of brokenness, rebellion, and decay. When we consider sin and its ramifications through close inspection of the Seven Deadly Sins, it is as if we have strolled through the gallery of human depravity. As I wrote this book, and as you have been reading it, the stories and images of each chapter paint a sorry and pitiful image of one of the

major symptoms of the brokenness of sin in our world. It's a
macabre and revolting gallery to stroll. To me, it's painful to look at
what we have done to our lives and our world. It is painful for me to
look at what these sins I love have done in my life and how they
have affected those around me. Yet, the gallery of fallenness invites
us in to take stock of the real effects of our sin, to shock us out of
minimalization and inattention.

If sin most often means "to miss the mark," we have no problem
finding examples of marks missed. Our daily metropolitan newspa-
pers run photos with news stories that expose us to the many pictures of sin. I am not attempting to take a piece out of the media. I
have worked in the industry and know what a tough job media people have. I am also not attempting to be some sort of fundamental-
ist voice that rains fire on everything in our culture. What I am
trying to say is that we live in a fallen world and the evidence is
everywhere.

Even two thousand years ago, life seemed ugly much of the
time. The Apostle Paul pleaded in one of his letters, "Who will free
me from this body of sin and death?" When we look at both our
outer and inner worlds, we see bad news everywhere. Out-of-control
people gun down fellow employees at an office, famous figures exalt greed, tabloids extol lust and infidelity.

I said earlier that we all innately desire to live lives of love. Yet,
the chaos and decay in which we live don't exactly inspire beauty
and love. In fact, they can make us despair that there is any possibility of redemption and witnessing the power of love.

This point of despair and the absence of self-help options are
actually good. I know, I'm a little postmodern and fancy decon-
structing and reconstructing things, but I think there's a good point
here.

You see, when we look at our lives and our world, hoping for
love but seeing the opposite, we become fully aware of our inade-

quacies. Like Paul, you and I throw up our hands asking who will deliver this world, who will deliver us from this life of sin and death? Is there really any way out of this mess?

Paul's answer to his rhetorical question is "Thanks be to God . . . Jesus Christ is here to save." In the context of the ugliness of this gallery of human depravity, it might be said, Jesus is a thing of extreme beauty. Jesus is the new aesthetic of a fallen world. In him, there is order yet freedom, a tenderness that can practice tough love and consecration to the values of heaven in the midst of an earth-bound world. And Jesus proved that humanity is capable of living out the fullness of what it means to be created in the image of God. In the Incarnation, the God who created us in His image creates Himself in our image. In Jesus, we see God doing a hands-on demonstration of what true humanity looks like. The beauty, justice, symmetry, and discipline of Jesus' life is absolutely captivating. Jesus' life as a human beckons us to follow him and become like him. What's fascinating to me is that the more I become aware of how weak and broken I am, the more I find myself crying out for a savior. I know I need help.

You see, the good thing about the messes in our lives and in our world is that they beckon us to look for a savior. And Jesus is quite up to the job. He is the picture of all that we long for and need. He is the epitome of love.

Spiritual masters write about the many "books" that lead us to God. One is the book of nature. Nature is the Creation as it is and as it can be. Mountains, lakes, oceans, clouds, wind, rain, and sunshine's warmth strike a chord deep inside us that says, "Yes. There is a God." As we contemplate the reality of God in nature, we rise just a little bit above the despair in which we live when our eyes are focused on the handiwork of humankind with all of its travesties.

Yet another book is the Book of Scripture. In the texts of the Old and New Testaments, we receive a revelation of God's values. God speaks to us. This is why Scripture is called the Word of God. Scripture is a historical account of God's attempt to be in a redemptive relationship with His whole Creation. Humanity has often shunned this pursuing God. But Scripture demonstrates God's earnestness right up to God Himself jumping into a bag of skin and bones in Jesus Christ.

The Book of Nature and the Book of Scripture push us into the contemplation of God. Who is God? What is God like? What does God think? How does God feel about the human race? Is God a personal God? As these questions arise, some of us feel that we are dealing with distant intangibles that have no answer. At this point, I have to say, thank God for God. Because Jesus Christ becomes the third book that tells us about God and leads us into a relationship with One who can save this world from sin and death.

A rock song a few years ago asked what it would be like if God became human and was with us. The writer of the song asked if God had a name and wondered if we could tell God's name to God's face. Well, in our Christian story, God does have a name, and a face. It's Jesus. We can address him by name. We can come to Him in prayer. We do have a champion of our cause and an advocate on our behalf.

The marvelous thing about Christ is that He is fully divine and fully human, the God-Man. Jesus can relate to the human condition and can relate to the things of heaven as a charter member of the Trinity. One poetic statement in the New Testament says of Jesus, "He is the visible image of the invisible God." Jesus is sometimes technically known as an economic representation of the Trinity. In other words, when God reveals God's self to humanity, He does it not as the three-in-one, but as Jesus. And Jesus so perfectly represents all of what God is and does, that His very nature and presence are all that is needed. If you've seen and contemplated Jesus, you know all there is about God.

There's another thing I want to mention about knowing God and progressing in our ability to love in the midst of a torn-up and sinful world. Knowing and loving God are not something that only theologians and Einstein-type brains can comprehend and achieve. It's much easier than that, mostly because God is reaching out to us and apprehending us. We don't find God. God finds us. Karl Barth, one of the great theological minds of all time, summed up this simplicity of the life of faith when he referred to God's attempts to communicate with us by nature, Scripture, and Jesus as "God talking baby-talk" with us.

If you are a bit of a dolt, like me, you will probably find this notion of simplicity encouraging. But while knowing God may seem simple, it can seem hard to accomplish in the midst of our complex and confusing lives.

For instance, I have always known that it is good for people to exercise. Once I get exercising, I really enjoy it and I feel the long-term positive effects. It's so simple, right? Wrong. I have trouble stringing days of exercise together let alone weeks, months, and years. And yet it's weeks, months, and years that are necessary to reap the benefits of exercise.

Moral and spiritual development follow the same track as exercise. The pilgrimage of faith to know God and receive God's absolute love is a long road. We don't get far overnight. We sometimes go backward. Like exercise, we sometimes feel that the pain and strain are not worth it.

There was a man with a terrible family history who was a part of a congregation I serve. He was at total enmity with his father. His dad died suddenly and the two were never reconciled. Over the next year or two, this gentleman was in deep pain wondering "what if" or blaming his father for all his problems. At the same time, he was sad as sad could be. Every Sunday during worship, he would melt down into tears and audible sobbing. After a while, he quit coming to church.

I called to inquire about him and he said that he had stopped coming to church because at church all of his issues and emotions surfaced in a powerful confluence of pathos. My gentle advice to this fellow was to keep at the worship. Let the tears flow. It sounded to me like the outrageous, healing love of God was tapping into the very center of this man's life. He was getting therapy and spiritual exercise beyond his wildest dreams. The pain is worth it if we understand it in the context of lifelong exercise.

The first step in this lifetime exercise is a little like stretching. You know how you try to loosen key muscles before you run, ski, walk, play tennis, or ride a bicycle. Those stretches make you ready, warm you up. Not only do they loosen muscles, but also they allow you to begin to focus on what's ahead in your exercise outing.

The classical understanding of Christian obedience is a stretch from our current comforts to a vision of who God is and what life with God can be. The first and foremost exercise of obedience is to show up in God's presence. When you and I commit the sins we love instead of receiving God's love for us, we play a little game that most of us are very good at. We pretend that God isn't there. We pray for the things we need, and we sense God's presence in a worship service, then when we have a fit of anger, we lie to ourselves and convince ourselves that God wasn't watching just then. We have a lust boil-over and rent a triple-X-rated video and try to pretend that God didn't see it.

Several years ago, I counseled a young man, Justin, who was having a terrible time with pornography and chronic masturbation. This fellow was a very gifted man with an important job and a vital relationship with God in Jesus Christ. Nothing that he seemed to do was helping conquer his problem.

In my office he said, "It makes me want to kill myself."

I asked him if he would take some advice from me. Justin said, "Anything."

I told him that he should continue in his normal life of prayer, but the next time he rented a porno movie and took it home, he should pray: "God, I know that this isn't right but I have terrible unmet needs for love and intimacy that I cannot address in any other way."

Justin burst in, "And you call yourself a pastor! How could you tell me to keep on doing this!"

He actually rose from his chair and was headed for the door when I said, "God already knows the needs you have in your heart and God has watched every single pornographic movie you have rented and witnessed every act of self-gratification that you have ever done. Why not stop pretending and acknowledge the God who is already there when you struggle with this stuff."

Justin left my office very upset with me. Several months later, he returned. His opening words were, "You were right. God is there with me. That recognition has spoiled lust for me and made me listen to the real yearnings for love that are in my heart."

Justin still struggles. But he's making progress.

I find it an interesting notion that we can bring God's presence to the places where we sin. In the light of God's loving presence the sins we love don't burn very brightly.

When we train ourselves to come into God's presence, we immediately find ourselves less distracted by the pictures of a world gone wrong. We become less fascinated by things sinful and are ashamed of our own sinfulness. While negative influences fade from our view, the ultimate positive image of God appears and captures us heart and soul.

Experiencing God's presence is the simple act of stopping and saying, "God, here I am. If you've got something for me, I'm listening. In the meantime, help me to learn to enjoy just being with you." Another thing we must understand about God's presence is that it is a loving, empowering, and inspiring presence. For those of us who are followers of Jesus Christ, our sins are forgiven. God isn't mad. God is wildly in love with each of us.

Yet as Christians, many of us have adopted an image of a God who is angry when we sin; a God who is waiting to punish us. Frankly, God doesn't need to punish us, our punishment is built into the sins we commit. Consequences of our lousy choices are enough judgment.

We must each make sure that our understanding of God includes His patient, sympathetic nature. We must face the absoluteness of God's love. No matter who we become, or what we do—good or bad—we cannot get God to love us any more or any less than He already does. This is great news. God is sold on you and me. God's presence in our lives is redemptive, positive, restorative, guiding. Get over the notion of an angry God. Too many of us sinners hold up the magnitude of our sin to a false image of an angry God and assume that we are cut off, damned, and hopeless. Such views lead persons to give up and give into their various vices rather than make progress against them.

The first and foremost step in living the life of love is living in the presence of a loving God. All other things follow. Right now, get ready to set this book down, and sit totally still for five minutes. Address God with the words, "Lord, I know you are here. I want to be with you." Then just sit still and let God's presence come into focus. Let God love you. This sort of access to God's power and love is the only true starting point for moving forward spiritually.

Prayer, worship, reading scripture, studying scripture, committed fellowship with other Christ-followers, and sacrificial service are secondary exercises. They come after the stretching of just being with God. I find it interesting that when Abraham, the first patriarch of the Old Testament, died, he was not lauded as a great leader, a great thinker, or a moral giant. He was none of these. His epitaph reads, "He was a friend of God." Now, if God created all that is and made us a part of Creation in order to know us intimately, don't you think being a friend of God is a worthy ambition—and an exciting source of meaning and purpose in life?

A courageous man named Ken lay in a hospital bed dying of a terrible form of cancer. He was a friend of the family and I was only a young man of eighteen. I had never stood at the bedside of a dying person and was understandably uncomfortable. He looked me and several other young people directly in the eyes and said, "God is what it's all about. Nothing else matters."

Albert Einstein was asked about the depth of his inquiries into the operation of the universe through mathematics and physics. His goal is often quoted: "I want to know God's thoughts. All else is details."

Getting nose to nose with God and stretching ourselves to be regularly in His presence is what it's all about. Anything we do or don't do after that is of much lesser value. For those of us who long to be remembered as friends of God, it is good news that God presents Himself to us as loving, accepting, and forgiving. We need not fear such a God.

Now, once we begin our spiritual exercises by developing intimacy with God in the presence of pure love, we can begin the cycle all over. We can go back to book one: the book of nature. In this second visit, we survey the wonder of what it is while in the presence of God. Our wows become articulations of worship and praise. And we not only see things we never saw before, but we see things that we have seen many times over much differently than ever before.

The Book of Scripture also comes to life in the presence of God when it is read and studied. The more carefully studied the better by my thinking. Scripture is objectively the Word of God, because it is revealed to the human community by the Spirit of God through the pens of prophets, kings, teachers, historians, and apostles.

While this notion of God's words as objective truth in a postmodern milieu that is suspicious of any claims of truth is encouraging, it seems anything but personal.

But the book of Scripture becomes personal when we look at it after we have stretched ourselves in the presence of God. Karl Barth was known for saying that Scripture is the Word of God, but it also becomes the living Word of God to each of us as we read it with eyes of faith and with the very present illumination of the Spirit of God.

It is very easy to objectify Scripture saying, "This is the Word of God." We focus all our attention on the object: We do studies of minuscule Greek words and haggle over the best rendering of texts. And yes, these activities show that we respect Scripture as the Word of God. But when it comes right down to making sense of life, objectifying Scripture separates us from the Source of life. What we really want is not to simply understand the biblical author's intent, but to have the Word jump to life as living words to you and me regarding our lives of faith.

I think this is the result of focusing on biblical literacy, with too little regard for allowing the Word of God become the words of God to us. We not only need to know the Scriptures. We need to meditate upon them and make them a part of who we are. One of the errors of evangelical Christianity is that we have settled for a prepositional faith without the existential or experiential aspect of faith that is so enormously valuable.

While knowing Scripture and doctrine are very important, we must also know the absolute reality of God's presence and power in our lives. We must experience our faith as well as think it.

When I am praying and stewing about a former boss whom I detest and who still troubles me, God's loving presence makes me feel a little silly about holding such a grudge. I don't feel ashamed, but I do feel amazed at my inability to move on. Following a time of meditation, during which I encountered my bittersweet self, I opened the New Testament to Paul's letter to the Romans. Now, I am not making this up—it really happened. The section of Scripture I read talked about making my life a "living sacrifice." I was truly inspired. I prayed, "God, I want my life to show this level of consecration. I want to give myself to you—body, soul, mind, and strength." Several verses later I read some applications on how to be a living sacrifice in which Paul said, "in so far as it is possible with you, be at peace with everyone." I want the sentimental consecration, but God trapped me into putting legs on my wishes. The objective Word of God as shared by Paul became the living and powerful Word of God to Randy that day and I began a serious process of letting go of my petty anger and bitterness. I couldn't have done it without God directly working with me.

In my contemplation of God, the Lord affirms a desire in me to be connected to the divine. In the Scripture, that desire is rekindled and verbalized by the invitation to present myself as a living sacrifice. In these two actions, God is showing me who I really want to be. Then I get hit by the words "insofar as it is possible with you, be at peace with everyone." Reading this line didn't defeat me. Rather, it made me want to throw off any impediment to knowing God more deeply as well as any hindrance to my own personal growth. To me, this is what happens when the Scriptures come alive by exercising reflection and holy imagination on the texts of Scripture while consciously being open to nudges from the ever-present God.

As I receive nudges about how to deal with my issues through the Scripture in the presence of Absolute Love, I cannot help but contemplate Jesus, who is the fully functional representation of God as applied to human life. As I work on my anger, I envision Jesus hanging innocently on the cross saying, "Forgive them, Father. They know not what they are doing." Things take on a new perspective. At this point I become spiritually, emotionally, and intellectually committed to Jesus as a model for humanity. This is how Jesus treats mistreaters: He forgives them. I found myself saying, "Jesus, if you forgive those who executed you wrongfully, I guess I can do it toward a boss who was objectionable to work with." Then I kept practicing the forgiveness.

Many young people these days wear necklaces or bracelets that say, "WWJD." This is an abbreviation for the question, "What Would Jesus Do?" My kids wear them. I support their use because it is a public symbol of commitment to Jesus Christ and His way that is the way of truth and life. The bracelets also remind people of who they are. They are not alone. They belong to God.

But there is one fallacy embodied in the WWJD bracelets. It's an inherent flaw easily overlooked. You see, for Christ-followers, it is not a matter of asking, "What would Jesus do?" as if we were contemplating the life of some dead guy. I wonder how Mozart would write this piece? I wonder how Gandhi would handle a justice issue we are facing in our neighborhood? How would Lincoln have behave during the civil rights movement?

The evil forces of this world tried to silence the voice and, once and for all, snuff out the life of Jesus in hopes that His beauty and perfection would be lost in the gristmill of time. But, oops! There was this funny thing that happened three days after Jesus was crucified. He conquered death as the Spirit of God raised the entirety of Jesus, including his physical body, from death. Scriptural accounts tell us that Jesus is alive and well, enthroned as Lord (boss) of the universe. It's not a matter of "What would Jesus do?" Really. It's a matter of "Jesus, what are you doing and what do you want me to do about it?"

We mustn't sentimentalize Jesus as some historical figure, confining Him to his grave, but rather allow our interactions with Him through the Holy Spirit to be intimate and transformational. He's with us. We don't conceive plans based upon what Jesus might do according to our speculation. Instead, we listen for a still small voice that is the Master, and we interact with that inner voice.

As we encounter Christ, we also encounter Christ's promise to be with us. This is a great promise. Are you a total sinner like me? Do you worry that God might abandon you? If so, take comfort in the fact that Jesus promises to be with us through the Holy Spirit. One Old Testament poem in the Book of Psalms says, "Even if I make my bed in hell, you are there with me, O God." You've got to like this God-with-us idea. But there's more.

God is also for us. He is our advocate. God oversees our destiny. God's disposition toward us is radical affirmation. In layman's terms, God is crazy about you and me. We looked at the completeness and perfection of God's love toward us earlier in this chapter.

To have God with us and for us is powerful. But even that is not the entire story, for God is also in us. God in us means, near to our hearts. God is resident in us in the presence of the Holy Spirit. Not only do we have a companion and a guide, but also a source of comfort and strength for the journey that comes from beyond ourselves.

All of our interaction with God infuses us with a new perspective on the very nature of love. And our first exercises of love, as we have been examining them so far, are exercises of God-love by human beings. Out of the understanding of love that we gain from God, we have God with us, for us, and in us shaping our character and reducing us to love in action. It's a wonderful distillation process.

Have you ever been asked, "What's your goal in life?" If so, what was your answer? I have wondered what my response would be on numerous occasions. The life and teachings of Jesus might give us some hints. In Matthew's Gospel a very astute young man once asked Jesus about ultimate goals. He wanted to know what was the greatest and foremost commandment in the law of God. He was asking Jesus to give His answer about the goal in life. Christ's answer was, "Love the Lord your God with all your heart, soul, mind and strength. Love your neighbor as yourself. The goal in life for all of us is love. To know the love of God, to radiate God's investment of love in each of us outward into our world. To love and accept ourselves as works in progress. Love is the goal."

Love is an action that occupies all of us when manifested correctly. In our devotion to God we seek to love God viscerally, from our emotional center—from the heart. We grow in learning to understand the depths of our psychological makeup and give ourselves to loving God from the essence of our person. We grow in love for God with a sharp intellect tuned to the study of God and the study of contemporary life. We also study ourselves and keep a correct assessment of who we are and where we are. And, we love God with our strength. This means to love God with our willful self. Loving God with our strength is applying courageous acts of the will to loving God. That may mean staying up late to pray. That may mean practicing forgiveness when the "want to" seems missing.

A holistic love for God—heart, soul, mind, and body—also connects us to and roots us in God's love. This is why Jesus broke life's goal into three parts: Love God totally. Love yourself. Love your neighbor. Loving God and experiencing the love that God has been lavishing on us since we were born sets us up to be able to love and accept ourselves, which in turn frees us to fully love and accept others.

Ultimately our worth is not measured in what we do, who we know, or how we behave. Our worth is derived from who knows us: God. The acceptance of God's loving knowledge of each of us frees us to experiment with loving ourselves in healthy ways.

Some time ago, I was in the locker room of an NFL team for postgame interviews. The public relations director of the team was stomping around making a fuss about all sorts of things. He told me to do what I needed to do and get out of the locker room. He challenged my need to be there, showing his aggression physically and verbally. I just couldn't figure out why he was behaving that way. The behavior he exhibited made me wonder what was going on.

I walked toward the locker room door and one of the players I knew well, who was also a Christian, told me that he had seen the PR guy getting on my case. He said, "He's sort of an insecure guy to begin with and I think he is feeling raw right now because the coach scolded him and kicked him out of the locker room during the coach's postgame remarks."

Well, suddenly things made sense to me. Because of the PR guy's sensitivity to rejection and insecurity over his value, he took the locker room ejection hard. Since he was experiencing a lack of acceptance, he instinctually tried to replicate his internal atmosphere of rejection with others. We all do this sort of stuff. I think that's why Jesus' words on the goal of life include a healthy understanding of what it means to love one's self.

I recently entered therapy for some issues I am dealing with. When a dear friend heard that I was setting aside time and money for counseling, he said, "That's wonderful. You're worth it." Think of it: You are worth it. You are worth loving. Our love deficiencies cause us to love sins that kill us. Love fulfillment has the reverse effect. Such absolute love helps us ignore invitations to sin.

Finally, we can begin to engage our world on a different level. "The only shocking act that remains in this world is love." And you and I inherit from God's Spirit within us the potential to live a life of shocking acts. We open ourselves to the practice which Jesus refers to as loving our neighbor as ourselves.

The path of love leads to and from God, to and from ourselves, and to and from others. It is a long and winding road with a variety of topographies. This is where the ever-present spirit of God becomes a unique asset. The Spirit builds virtues in us and gives us wisdom on the application of those virtues to the various life situations we encounter.

Remember our study of the fruit of the Spirit from Paul's letter to the Galatians? Paul says, "The fruit of the Spirit is love." The Spirit is reducing you and me to love. To live in God's spirit is to walk in the pathway of love. Paul goes on to describe the various manifestations of love as "joy, peace, patience, kindness, goodness, faithfulness, gentleness, and self-control."

I mentioned earlier in this book an old Jesus People song with the lyrics "Jesus reduce me to love." It is a plea to become like the One whom we love and lavish time upon. It is a plea to replicate the character of God in God's creatures.

Reduction to love is the ability to view life through a lens of love and to shape belief systems, values, actions, and character that exude love in all its forms.

The fruit of the Spirit is love with legs on. Joy is a deep and abiding sense of the beauty in life. Peace is a sense of being whole and correctly deployed in life. Patience is the ability to trust God and wait for the right answers. Kindness is the predisposition to treat someone else well simply because they exist. Goodness, or liberality, means sharing of self in proper ways. Faithfulness means keeping ourselves centered in our faith. Gentleness teaches us about our relationships. It shapes sensitivity in us and beckons us to treat others as we wish to be treated. In times of tension, we push no harder than necessary. And self-control means mastering passions so that we are a slave to no one but Christ, whose leadership yoke is easy and whose burdens are bearable by the grace of God.

The meditation upon fruitfulness brings us to a deeper knowledge of what God's spirit is shaping in you and me. But let's not forget one important fact that we have visited numerous times in this book—we cannot do it alone. Good fruit comes from good roots.

So much of what I have been stressing in this book about the entanglement of sin has redirected us to our roots as children of God. Every orchard tender knows that weak roots grow weak trees and pathetic fruit. The spiritual exercises of love deepen and strengthen our roots.

Several years ago, I was taken on a helicopter tour of a local forestry giant's properties. My special trip focused on forest replenishment. I got to see how enhanced techniques took Douglas firs from seedling to harvest in about thirty years. These trees grow bigger and faster than natural growth timber, and it's not strange chemicals that account for the growth. Rather, it is careful attentiveness to enhancing the ways of nature that creates such a positive result.

At one point in the tour, our guide led us out into a huge field of two- and three-year-old trees. He explained that the first year of a Douglas fir's life was spent at an indoor nursery. And its next several years were spent in the field. Then, at the right time, the trees were transplanted to the forest and allowed to grow naturally. Giving the trees this head start gave them protection from animal and severe weather damage.

As we were about to move on, the guide pointed to a tractor pulling something that looked like the sled that baseball groundskeepers use to drag the infield. He said, "That machine is a wrencher." He then explained that when a group of trees in the field hits two years old, the wrencher is driven down its row. The wrencher slices underground and cuts the taproot and all the other roots off several inches under the ground. The wrencher then literally lifts the tree up out of the ground and drops it back down on top of its original hole where it is allowed to resume its growth.

The wrenching process stimulates the growth of new roots, a thicker taproot, and a broader root base. Fruitfulness is all about roots and these tree-growing people understood that if the tree's roots were exercised and stimulated to deepen, broaden, and multiply, the tree would grow more successfully.

I don't know about you, but I have had some wrenching experiences. The sizzling psychic pain of rejection. The loss of loved ones. Health issues like my diabetes. Man, these things hit with force. They slash at our roots. They cut us off from the comforts we know. Sometimes we're not sure we'll survive the wrenching experiences of life that pick us up and set us down in unlikely places.

Wrenching is not fun, but it's necessary for strength and growth. We desire fruitful lives. Wrenching gives us a greater capacity to soak in the nutrients of the Holy Spirit. Wrenching helps us better access absolute love and makes us stronger to walk the path of love.

You and I wrestle with pride by thinking we are better. We wrestle with envy over what others have and do. We battle fiery bouts of anger when we are threatened. Our despondent moments beckon us to a couch potato existence of sloth. We want to own the world, so we unleash greed. We want to consume all there is and gluttony becomes our field marshal. And we want to be passionate people, but we minimize our passion by focusing it solely on sex, thus becoming victims of lust.

The answer to living with and around these constant sources of danger is to walk the path of love. And it all starts with good roots.

Sin Spotting

This book was written for you and me—hard-core sinners. It is a compilation of the sins *we* love. It's all about your struggle and my struggle. My fervent prayer is that both you and I will gain access to spiritual resources that fight against these seven deceitful and destructive categories of sin. It is also my hope that you and I begin to reflect more and more virtue in the form of the fruit of the Spirit.

One of my great fears in writing a book about sin is that people would read it and "use it" on others. Please, give me a break. Don't roll this book up and slap others across the bridge of the nose with it in some sort of a "Bad dog!" gesture.

In the New Testament, the Apostle Paul has some great insights into sin. At one point he says, "If anyone you know is caught in a sin, you who are truly spiritual restore them fully . . . oh, and be careful that you yourself don't get tripped up by this deceitful thing called sin."

The word that Paul uses for sin in this particular text is *paraptoma*. It means "to slip." What a gracious notion. If you see someone sin and hurt others and damage their own lives, try to see it as a slip.

I spent my first semester of college on an eastern Washington campus that froze over in November and thawed in April. School started in late September, and it wasn't long before snow covered the entire campus.

The walkways of this school have since been heated. But back in antiquity when I attended, the sidewalks were notorious for slick patches of ice, concealed under new-fallen snow.

Stepping onto an ice patch was sudden agony. Your legs would fly out, you would slam down on your rear, and your textbooks would go flying. No matter how you walked, in spite of all caution, these ice patches still could find you and toss you to your backside with ease.

This sort of slipping has a lifelong impact. I have never carried a wallet in my back pocket since I was eighteen. When you have received a wallet-shaped bruise on your gluteus maximus, you just automatically change your routine.

This image of slipping on hidden ice and being damaged is exactly the image Paul is using for sin. We are so prone to it, the environment is so prepared for it, that, sometimes, we just step wrong and down we go.

Paul doesn't recommend lashing out at the person. Rather, he envisions an offer to pick up the wounded ones, help them dust off, collect themselves, and get back on with the business of life.

Those of us who are really growing spiritually on the path of love will find ourselves condemning the sins of others less and less while practicing compassion and support as much as possible.

Paul reminds us that when we see someone overtaken by sin, we have to be careful, because there is a slippery spot waiting right up ahead of us. No one would have seen someone slip on the ice at my frozen college campus, mock him or her, then start running at a sprint through the snow. That would have been an invitation to several weeks in traction.

But we Christians have become known as the only army in the world that kills its wounded. We deal with sins as if they are something that God has never seen and would be embarrassed about. We hide and rationalize our own internal bent for evil by decrying the evils of society or other persons.

Please, do yourself, me, and a watching world that displays bumper stickers like "Jesus, save me from your people" a favor by using the contents of this book to inform your own journey. And as it regards others, use the content of this book to develop empathy and sensitivity to your sin-sickened fellow human beings.

APPENDIX

Vices and Virtues Chart

After all of the work we have been doing with virtues and vices, I thought it important to develop a grid for personal reflection. The left-hand column is one of the Seven Deadly Sins, the center column is the fruit of the Spirit manifestations that apply to that sin, and the right-hand column is Aristotle's list of the seven classical virtues which correspond.

Let love rule!

SEVEN DEADLY SINS	PAUL'S FRUIT OF THE SPIRIT	ARISTOTLE'S VIRTUES
Pride	Kindness	Righteousness
Envy	Joy	Great-spiritedness
Anger	Gentleness	Gentleness
Sloth	Faithfulness	Courage
Greed	Peace/Goodness	Liberality
Gluttony	Self-control	Sobriety
Lust	Patience/self-control	Self-control